Contemporary Rugs

Christopher Farr
Matthew Bourne &
Fiona Leslie

Contemporary Rugs

Art and Design

MERRELL

First published 2002 by
Merrell Publishers Limited
42 Southwark Street
London SE1 1UN

Telephone +44 (0)20 7403 2047
E-mail mail@merrellpublishers.com

Publisher: Hugh Merrell
Editorial Director: Julian Honer
Art Director: Matthew Hervey
Managing Editor: Anthea Snow
Production Manager: Kate Ward
Editorial & Production Assistant: Emily Sanders

Copyright © Christopher Farr and
Matthew Bourne 2002

Distributed in the USA by Rizzoli International
Publications, Inc. through St. Martin's Press,
175 Fifth Avenue, New York, NY 10010

British Library Cataloguing-in-Publication Data:
Farr, Christopher
    Contemporary Rugs: art and design
    1.Rugs – Design 2.Rugs – History –
    20th century 3.Textile designers
    I.Title II.Bourne, Matthew III.Leslie, Fiona
    746.7'904

ISBN 1 85894 164 4

Designed by Brighten the Corners –
    Studio for Design
Edited by Richard Dawes

Printed and bound in Spain

Front jacket: Verner Panton, *Square Rug*,
handknotted wool rug, produced in 2000
by Christopher Farr, London, UK, from an
original design of 1969 (detail, see p. 158).
Courtesy of Marianne Panton.

Page 2: Kate Blee, *River*, 2001, handwoven-
flatweave wool rug, designed for
Christopher Farr, London, UK.

Page 6: Brad Davis and Janis Provisor,
Grid, 1998, handknotted wild-silk rug,
designed for Fort Street Studio, Hong
Kong, China.

Pages 8–9: Angela Adams, *Manfred*, 1999,
gun-tufted wool rug, produced by Angela
Adams, Maine, USA.

Pages 46–47: Michael Sodeau, *Red Rug*
and *Blue Rug*, 2000, handmade looped-pile
wool rugs, produced by Christopher Farr,
London, UK. The triangular formers convert
the rugs into loungers.

Pages 192–93: Marcel Zelmanovitch,
Untitled, 1992, handknotted wool rug,
produced by Galerie Diurne, Paris, France.
One of three rugs commissioned for
La Grande Arche de la Défense, Paris.

Contents

Foreword

What is a rug? It is, in fact, quite reasonable to ask such
a question. Of course, sometimes the answer comes as
a lovely surprise, as in the discovery that one is tramping
over a genuine work of art without the slightest remorse
or soul-searching about one's right to do so.

A rug can emit a signal. It can suggest and define a space.
Its luxurious pile can be an invitation to stretch out on the
floor. Its proportions are significant.

Recently I noticed in a deluxe but nonconformist hotel that
the rooms provided high, wooden, ivory-lacquered beds,
each with a simple, rectangular carpet beneath that created
a comfort zone. Here was a visual pleasure offering balance
and harmony – and no further need for bedside rugs.

I like to see a rug floating on a neutral-coloured ground,
like an island. One suggestion: try not to introduce too much
furniture into the same space. It is important to allow the
rug to fulfil its rôle of enhancing the general context, whether
modest or magnificent, to be inviting yet independent of its
function, to create a grammar for, or to punctuate, the
environment. The essential basis for any effective interior
is flexibility, and rugs will always reverberate the weakness
or strength of the whole concept.

Respect them!

Andrée Putman
Paris, 2002

A Century of Rug Design

1. Charles Rennie Mackintosh, *Design for the Dining Room in an Art Lover's House*, published in *Haus Eines Kunst-Freundes*, in the series *Meister Der Innen-Kunst*, II, by Hermann Muthesius, Darmstadt 1901.

2. Mackay Hugh Baillie Scott, *Water-colour of the Music Room in a house at Crowborough*, in *The Studio Yearbook of Decorative Art*, XXVI, London 1902.

Introduction

During the past century the unique handwoven rug[1] has continued to enjoy a special place in the decorative arts of Western Europe and the United States. Coming out of a centuries-old tradition as an object of luxury and beauty, admired and coveted for its excellence in both execution and appearance, it nevertheless originated as a product of practical necessity. This dual nature is one of the reasons for the fascination with rugs in the twentieth and twenty-first centuries. Rugs create a "tension between the qualities of an object made for everyday use and a work of art sensual [and] tactile"[2] and pose the question of whether they are floor coverings for underfoot comfort, decorative elements of interior design or works of art.

The presence of a rug in a room is a statement in itself. With the development, over the past 150 years, of wall-to-wall carpeting and mass-production techniques, handmade area carpets and rugs have become more distinctive, and now, at the beginning of the twenty-first century, they command attention and status, whether in a domestic interior, a corporate office, an embassy or a place of worship. The best-quality rugs are still luxury items, and the choice to have a unique rug or carpet with a particular type of weave and design says much about the person who commissioned it and about his or her lifestyle and taste in design. The exclusivity of owning an expensive, unique product means that rugs and carpets are often seen as lavish and esoteric items, but original designs are, in fact, gradually becoming more affordable and accessible to a wider market.

The presence of rugs and carpets makes a significant impact on an interior. Both the warmth of the materials and the effects of the colours, whether subtle or bright, dark or light, can change the mood of a room and the people in it. Rugs are sometimes used to reinforce the architectural structure of a room, and many designers in the twentieth century, particularly proponents of the Modern Movement, emphasized this relationship in their rectilinear rug patterns. Naturally, rugs have to compete for attention with other furnishings and decorative objects. The catalogue of an exhibition of rugs held in New York in 1929 stated that designers "aim apparently to make the rug the most conspicuous decorative object in a room",[3] and it was said later that the rugs of the important 1930s American designer Marion Dorn "kept one's eyes riveted on the floor".[4] Rugs enhance the decoration of a room and, since the eighteenth century, have been a key element in complete design schemes, in which walls, floors and furnishings, as well as individual objets d'art, were co-ordinated in colour and style.

A further use of rugs and carpets is to define the areas of social activity within a space, and to clarify where people are expected to move around, stop and gather. Whether alone or in social situations, we are drawn to a rug, attracted by its design, its colours or the tactility of its materials and finish. Rugs and carpets are often placed under groupings of furniture, for example a dining-table and chairs (fig. 1), or used in a living-room where seating and a television are gathered together. Alternatively they can be scattered around a room at the points where people enter, stop to open a cupboard or sit in a chair (fig. 2). Area carpets can also delineate a space that is intended to be open and uncluttered by objects. The prominent French designer Andrée Putman has stated that she sees rugs as small islands "which can be partly occupied or, on the contrary, totally free from furniture or objects".[5] The thick pile of a woollen rug also affects the general pace of movement in a space as people slow down to enjoy the soft, sinking feeling underfoot, as opposed to rushing across a hardwood or linoleum-covered floor.

Rugs can be inviting and encourage informal lounging on floors, although sometimes an example looks so beautiful that it can discourage any human contact that might disturb its aesthetic presence. The removal of shoes to walk on a rug is a mark of respect for the designer, weaver and dyer. The feel of the pile is luxurious, and the sensuous properties of woven wool and silk cannot be ignored in a rug lying seductively on a floor. It could be argued that, at the beginning of the twenty-first century, in a world where human contact is declining, we create objects that go some way towards fulfilling that sensuous need.

Finally, handwoven rugs and carpets inherently possess a strong sense of history. Contemporary examples are part of a long continuum joining the past with the present and the future, but, as Cornelia Bateman Faraday, the pioneer in the history of carpets, has said, they should above all "express absolutely the spirit of their times".

1900–1909: New Styles for a New Century

3. Anonymous, Viennese Art Nouveau carpet, c. 1905, handknotted wool, possibly produced by Joh. Backhausen & Sohne, 345 x 251 cm (136 x 99 in.).

In the first decade of the twentieth century the design and manufacture of rugs in Western Europe and the United States underwent dramatic changes. Industrialization of the techniques for manufacturing rugs and carpets had been perceived by various concerned individuals and parties, including the Art-Workers' Guild and the Arts and Crafts Exhibition Society, to be having negative effects on both the standard of production and aesthetic qualities. The resulting efforts by some to temper, or at least influence, the making and appearance of rugs was effective at the top end of the market, eventually permeating the wider market in a diluted form.

One of the key figures to influence twentieth-century rug design was William Morris (1834–1896). The force and conviction of his ideas, although firmly set in nineteenth-century Britain, were felt by many design movements in both Europe and the United States long into the twentieth century. The leading figure of the British Arts and Crafts Movement, Morris was fervently against industrialization and what he and others saw as a decline in the standard of materials, processes and the resulting goods, as well as the undesirable effects on the people making and using these. Above and beyond his socialist inclinations and concerns, he encouraged his fellow designers and artists to revert to a more craft-based and handmade way of rug and textile production, which he also defended on aesthetic grounds. In the leaflet of the first exhibition of rugs and carpets by his firm, Morris & Co., in 1880, he proclaimed that: "... for the future, we people of the West must make our own hand-made carpets ...; and ... these, while they should equal the Eastern ones as nearly as may be in materials and durability, should by no means imitate them in design, but show themselves obviously to be the outcome of modern and Western ideas, guided by those principles that underlie all architectural art in common."

This is not to say that Morris rejected Eastern types. Indeed, he greatly admired sixteenth- and seventeenth-century Persian rugs and owned examples himself. He was also interested in medieval and Italian Renaissance textile patterns that had simple repeat elements.[6] Morris fervently studied the techniques of rug-making and learnt to weave on the loom, redeveloping natural dyes in preference to using modern, bright, artificial versions. From 1878 he set up various weaving enterprises to challenge and change the direction of contemporary rug and carpet production, which he believed was then in decline.

Morris and his fellow designers, such as C.F.A. Voysey (1857–1941), Walter Crane (1845–1915) and Lewis Foreman Day (1845–1910), were also concerned with carpet patterns. Above all, Morris was adamant that a rug, the primary function of which was to lie on the floor and be walked upon, should be flat and have no illusionistic three-dimensional devices or trompe l'œil effects creating a false ground. As a result, the designs of Morris and his associates displayed a simplification of pattern, an economy of line and a flattening of depth. They were also characterized by the frequent use of green grounds, which were not commonly found in Persian or Oriental rugs.[7] The early results of Morris's campaign could be seen at the Arts and Crafts Exhibition Society, founded in 1888, which was the main forum for designers working in a broad range of craft-based media and in a similar spirit to Morris. The society's first show exhibited mainly handwoven carpets as well as some machine-woven examples by John Templeton & Co., a progressive carpet manufacturer in Glasgow. Unfortunately, the high cost of putting Morris's ideas into action led to his having little direct

4. C.F.A. Voysey, *Donnemara* Donegal
carpet, *c.* 1903, handknotted wool,
produced for Liberty, 366 x 251 cm
(144 x 99 in.).

influence on industrial production, but his
fellow designers and architects took them
to heart and carried them across the world.
This quite unique communication with
other designers and organizations working
in related fields at this time set the scene
for a cross-pollination of ideas across
Europe and the United States, the result of
which was the flowering of the many forms
of Art Nouveau and then International
Modern (Modernist architecture before
World War II).

C.F.A. Voysey was one of the key
figures who carried the essence of Morris's
work into the twentieth century. As an
architecturally trained designer he used
bold decoration in his interiors and had a
great interest in flat-pattern design. His
strong personal style was a fusion of Arts
and Crafts influences, vernacular styles
and Art Nouveau, and manifested itself in
patterns of large, simplified floral and leaf
forms, as in his Donegal carpets such as the
Donnemara (fig. 4), which was mentioned
in the Liberty catalogue of 1903. Voysey's
famous *River Mat* of 1903, decorated with
scenes from rural life, is typical of his
frequent drawing upon figurative motifs
from the countryside to create furnishing
patterns. Another progressive rug
designer at this time was Walter Crane,
whose sinewy, lyrical style, heralding
Art Nouveau, was found in the rugs he
designed for John Templeton & Co. in
Glasgow in the 1880s. A founder member
of both the Art-Workers' Guild in 1884
and the Arts and Crafts Exhibition Society,
Crane had extensive contacts with
sympathetic organizations outside the
British Isles, and was an honorary member
of the important Vienna Secession in
Austria. He toured the East coast of the
United States in the early 1890s, showed
work in Budapest in 1900 and in Vienna in
1902, and in the same year exhibited at the
*Esposizione Internazionale d'Arte Decorativa
Moderna* in Turin, Italy.

Another rug-weaving producer was the Century Guild, founded in 1882 by Arthur Heygate Mackmurdo (1851–1942). Influenced by Morris and the Romantic philosopher and critic John Ruskin (1819–1900), this co-operative designed household furnishings, including rugs. Mackmurdo developed a distinctive style of his own and is seen as one of the originators of international continental Art Nouveau, influencing other designers, such as Voysey and Henry Clemens van de Velde. C.R. Ashbee (1863–1942) was one of the driving forces behind Arts and Crafts as an internationally influential movement. After founding the Guild and School of Handicraft at Toynbee Hall, east London, in 1888, he later collaborated with the Vienna Secession and in 1910 travelled to the United States, where he met Frank Lloyd Wright and was greatly impressed by the American architect's work and philosophy. George Walton (1867–1933), after spending the first decade of his career in Glasgow, moved to London in 1897 to carry out interior-design commissions for a number of Kodak photographic shops throughout Europe. A strong proponent of Arts and Crafts, he produced designs that ranged from standard figurative, Turkish-derived compositions to more progressive abstract patterns of stylized floral motifs.

Archibald Knox (1864–1933) was a key proponent of the Celtic Revival of the 1890s to about 1910. He developed distinctive compositions with Celtic-derived motifs that were common to both his rug designs and the metalwork pieces he provided for Liberty. Another supplier of designs for the London store was the Silver Studio. Headed first by Arthur Silver (1853–1896) and then by his son Reginald Silver (also known as Rex Silver, 1879–1964), this studio played an important role in London in the first decades of the twentieth century, commissioning both well-established and less well-known designers who supplied designs for textiles, flat patterns and graphics for the commercial manufacturing market in Britain.

One of the most dynamic rug designers at this time was Frank Brangwyn (1867–1956). The Belgian-born, English-trained artist-designer started his long and broad career in the 1880s, designing tapestries in William Morris's weaving workshop. With a style strongly informed by his baptism in the Arts and Crafts Movement, he designed rugs covered from edge to edge with detailed intricate patterns, delighting in the trailing forms of Art Nouveau, before progressing to the more geometric, regulated compositions of Art Deco. From the early years of the century he produced designs for handknotted rugs for Alexander Morton's workshops in Donegal, Ireland, and chenille carpets for John Templeton & Co. in Glasgow. Brangwyn also designed for galleries in Paris, and examples such as the striking *The Vine* handknotted rug for La Maison de l'Art Nouveau show his characteristic boxy form, which was a synthesis of late Arts and Crafts with Celtic forms and Art Nouveau. A truly international designer from the beginning of the century, he worked in Britain, Paris and the United States.

In Scotland and Ireland quite different styles emerged from similar intentions. Scottish designers were, like the Isle of Man-born Archibald Knox, more drawn to Celtic and Scandinavian traditional motifs and forms. This can be seen clearly in the work of designers of the Glasgow School, such as Charles Rennie Mackintosh (1868–1928), Mackay Hugh Baillie Scott (1865–1945), Margaret and Frances Macdonald (1865–1933; 1874–1921) and Herbert McNair (1870–1945). The Celtic forms lent themselves easily to the lyrical, elegant expression in pattern design that was an early manifestation of the Art Nouveau style, which was eagerly taken up and further developed in Vienna and Belgium. Mackintosh was one of the major proponents of a restrained form of Art Nouveau, and the simplicity in composition and colour of his works has led them to be considered by many to be proto-Modernist. The architect-designer travelled in Italy in 1891 and later in Finland, which in part explains the Scandinavian tendencies in his rug designs. These are characterized by a minimalist, sparse pattern on a pale, soft ground, and the linearity of the boxy forms, as in the rugs for the Hill House commission in Helensburgh, Scotland, are architectural in context. Mackintosh's carpets in the Room de Luxe of the Willow Tea Rooms in Glasgow are decorated with two lines of small squares in well-spaced linear arrangements over larger white squares at greater intervals with, between them, variegated-width stripes defining walkways. In contrast there are long, sweeping, restrained foliate forms with simple, stylized flower heads, as in his design for a dining-room rug shown in the *House of an Art Lover* by the German architect and designer Hermann Muthesius (1861–1927), published in 1901 (fig. 1). In the second volume of the same series Mackay Hugh Baillie Scott's rugs were typical of his more medieval, craft-derived style: small rugs, or mats, and hall runners placed in convenient spots on bare wood floors and usually decorated with large, geometric, neo-Gothic motifs in a colour range based on natural greens and blues. They were widely featured in art and design journals such as *The Studio* (fig. 2). Both Mackintosh and Baillie Scott created rugs that essentially integrated with their complete interior schemes rather than existing in their own right.

Rug and carpet production was greatly aided by the services of two of the most progressive carpet manufacturers in Britain at the time. John Templeton & Co. and Alexander Morton & Co. were textile firms

5. Dun Emer, *c.* 1902, handknotted wool runner, 252 x 91.5 cm (99 x 36 in.).

that both commissioned and produced carpets for others, employing imaginative, progressive designs executed using both handknotting and machine-weaving techniques. As well as its factory in Carlisle, Morton's had set up, with the help of Irish government funding, several workshops for handknotted carpet-weaving works in Darvel, Killybegs and other villages in County Donegal, Ireland. Typical of the output of the Donegal workshops were rugs with large Persian and Turkish-derived, foliate forms and pieces in the more vernacular Irish-Celtic tradition with repeat patterns of stylized motifs.

Morton & Co. was not alone for long in Ireland. In 1902 the Dun Emer Guild was set up outside Dublin by Evelyn Gleeson (1855–1944), who had been trained in all aspects of carpet design and production at the South Kensington Schools of Design in London. With a thorough grounding in the teachings of Morris's Arts and Crafts ideals, she established a workshop with members of the embroidery school of May Morris (Morris's daughter) at Dundrum to instruct local girls in the techniques of handknotted carpet-weaving. The weaving workshops were part of a deliberate intention by Gleeson to promote Irishness and the Irish language, and the Dun Emer Guild also operated a printing press that specialized in publications in Gaelic. Dun Emer carpet designs were mainly derived from traditional Gaelic decorative forms and medieval manuscript illuminations, but also incorporated Turkish stylized motifs, in an effort to be "conspicuously Irish and new in design" (fig. 5).[8] During the first decade of the century other small-scale workshops were established in various parts of Ireland, but, despite the fact that the industry's profile was raised by exhibitions across Europe and in the United States from the beginning of the century, there was never, unfortunately, a successful commercial level of rug-making in Ireland.[9]

At the turn of the twentieth century, Paris was unique in being at the centre of both the avant-garde art scene and the luxury-goods market in Western Europe. Highly crafted goods, old and new, drew designers and buyers alike, and the Parisian market was epitomized by luxury handwoven rugs designed by distinguished artists. The city was a melting-pot of design trends in traditional historicism, International Modern and Art Nouveau, as well as reflecting influences from the newly annexed French colonies in Africa. The Exposition Universelle of 1900, held in Paris, was a showcase to the world and attracted designers and artists from Europe, the United States and Japan who were hungry for new and inspirational experiences at the start of the new century. In the field of rugs this resulted in the stimulation and proliferation of innovative and exciting new designs.

At the beginning of the century in Paris, and for the next thirty years, rugs were mainly the interest of the *décorateurs* and *ensembliers* (interior decorators and designers), of whom there were an established few. Numerous examples were also designed by known painters, sculptors and fashion designers. For many of these, designing rugs was a passing experiment, while for others it was one of their main professional activities. At this time most French-designed rugs were made in France, although a few were produced in Austria. What was also remarkable in this field, compared with other areas of creative interior design, was the number of female designers who developed successful careers.

The influence of Diaghilev's Ballets Russes later in the decade cannot be underestimated. After the company's first performances in Paris, in 1909, the dancers' bright and often surreal costumes did not go ignored by artists and designers in Western Europe. At this time modern rugs had more status in France than in most other countries, and there was a market for journals such as *Tapis Modernes* (*Modern Carpets*), which was published in the first years of the century.

Similar circumstances and events to those in France were bringing about changes in rug design in Belgium, Austria and Germany, although these countries were more open to outside influences and embraced Art Nouveau to a much greater degree, as well as accepting the more linear forms of early Modernism. While Belgian designers experienced much the same influences as their Parisian counterparts, they did not venture far into the more highly decorative and historical French tendencies, instead concentrating on the economical and lyrical aspects of the new style, Art Nouveau. Henry Clemens van de Velde (1863–1957), an Antwerp-born painter and architect who became a decorative designer, was strongly influenced by William Morris, and, at the end of the 1890s and during the early years of the new century, was working in true Art Nouveau. Also active at different times in Germany, The Netherlands and Paris, he saw the purity of form in design and architecture as key to his rug designs.

In Vienna, Otto Wagner (1841–1918), who, from 1894, directed the architecture department at the Akademie der bildenden Künste, was one of the foremost Viennese proponents of the Art Nouveau style, working in a curvilinear form. His protégés included Josef Maria Olbrich (1867–1908), Koloman Moser (1868–1918) and Josef Hoffmann (1870–1956), who were all founding members of the radical and highly influential Wiener Sezession (Vienna Secession), which was created as a rebellious gesture in 1897. They, too, designed carpets that were in the Viennese tradition of rich colours and patterns, in both the Art Nouveau manner and early transitional expressions of International Modern.

Hoffmann, born and trained in Moravia, finished his architectural training in Vienna. A founding member, in 1903, of the Wiener Werkstätte (Vienna Workshops), he was involved with the 1900 Exposition Universelle in Paris, designing the rooms for the Secession and Vienna's Kunstgewerbeschule (Arts and Crafts School), where he taught. Inspired by British Arts and Crafts, particularly the Guild of Handicrafts, he remained in close contact with Mackintosh and the Glasgow School of Art as well as the Modern Movement that was developing across mainland Europe. His designs were often of a linear style, with boxy motifs covering the whole surface, and many of his carpets were made by the textile manufacturer Joh. Backhausen & Söhne (fig. 3). Unlike Mackintosh, he used warmer, brighter colouring, such as pink-reds, in the Viennese tradition.

The rug designs of Otto Prutscher (1880–1949) were also striking in their brilliant, though discreet, colouring, and were decorated with delicate, elegant geometric patterns of triangles and lines. A student of Hoffmann, Prutscher started designing textiles, among other things, for the Wiener Werkstätte soon after their foundation. In 1909 a more architectonic, simply composed, highly detailed carpet was executed by Herrberger & Rhomberg.

In Munich, Art Nouveau, known from 1896 as Jugendstil, was characterized by the use of extremely sinuous lines and the abstraction of natural forms. The course of rug design in Germany was shaped by the founding in 1907 of first the Deutscher Werkstätte (German Workshops) and then the Deutscher Werkbund (German Art Union), which were influenced by the earlier developments of the British Arts and Crafts Movement. The founding members were advocates of reconciling art, design and industry and included Peter Behrens (1868–1940), Richard Riemerschmid (1868–1957) and the architect-designer

Bruno Paul (1874–1968), all of whom designed rugs, and Hermann Muthesius. The last of these designers had spent from 1896 to 1903 in Britain on behalf of the German government as 'attaché for architecture', studying industrial design and the applied arts, and was particularly struck by the work of Mackintosh and Baillie Scott of the Glasgow School. In Dresden, Gertrude Kleinhempel (1875–1948), who designed and taught textile design, was one of the few female textile designers in Germany to receive recognition at this time. Around 1909 a number of her well-balanced, visually stimulating geometric carpets were executed by the Werkstätten für Deutschen Hausrat (Workshops for German Household Interiors) under Theophil Müller in Dresden-Striesen, and some other gun-tufted Smyrna examples were made by the Wurzner Carpet Manufacturing Co.

In the United States the highest-profile rug designer was the architect Frank Lloyd Wright (1867–1959). Embodying the Arts and Crafts-derived philosophy that art should be incorporated into everyday life, his rugs had an architectural as well as practical and decorative uses. They were used to define living spaces in his open-plan interior schemes, where they reflected the architecture of the progressive offices and houses, such as the Prairie houses, which he was designing at the time. Such rugs typically had plain grounds and no borders, and the simple, linear patterns complemented the long, flat forms of the rugs and referred to the walls and ceiling. Wright's significant influence on rug design was felt throughout the United States and Europe from the early years of the decade.

1910s–1930s: The Flourishing Years

6. Duncan Grant for Omega Workshops, 1913, handknotted wool rug on a string warp, probably produced by the Wilton Royal Carpet Factory Ltd, 274 x 226 cm (108 x 89 in.).

7. Marion Dorn, c. 1930, handknotted woollen-pile rug on a jute warp, produced by the Wilton Royal Carpet Factory Ltd, 138 x 197 cm (54 x 78 in.).

8. (opposite) Marion Dorn, 1934, handknotted woollen-pile rug on a jute warp, produced by the Wilton Royal Carpet Factory Ltd, 208 x 122 cm (82 x 48 in.).

In Britain from the 1910s to the end of the 1930s some of the most progressive rug designs came from the Omega Workshops, formed in June 1913 by Roger Fry (1866–1934). Fry brought together a group of young avant-garde artists, including Duncan Grant (1885–1978), Frederick Etchells (1886–1973) and Vanessa Bell (1879–1961), with the intention of fusing art and interior design. They were heavily influenced by the art and design scene in Paris, and particularly by avant-garde movements such as Cubism and the Fauves and workshop precedents such as Paul Poiret's Atelier Martine, which had opened two years earlier. Omega produced domestic wares decorated in painterly, abstract forms. Duncan Grant's striped rug in bright, bold colours (fig. 6) was one of the first rugs available from Omega and was displayed on the Omega Sitting Room stand at the *Ideal Home Exhibition* in 1913. Although this rug is more rigid and geometric in pattern than most of Omega's characteristically florid style, Grant's use of bright colours heavily outlined with dark tones or black is a typical example of Omega's surface pattern on furniture, and it can also be seen in Vanessa Bell's early, geometric, Futurist-influenced rug of 1913 designed for Lady Hamilton.[10] Omega's work was too radical for most British taste and was particularly frowned upon by proponents of the early Arts and Crafts Movement.[11] It failed to develop a wide enough clientele to survive World War I and closed in 1919, the same year, ironically, in which the Bauhaus workshops opened in Germany.

Of a less painterly inclination, Ambrose Heal (1872–1959) was, in the early 1920s, designing Modernist rugs of a simpler type that depicted typically Scandinavian patterns with orderly grids of squares within squares on pale-cream backgrounds.[12] At this time his shop, Heal & Son Ltd, in Tottenham Court Road in central London, was one of the city's most progressive

furniture and interiors shops and continued to be at the forefront of contemporary design well into the 1960s.

Two major figures in British rug design in the 1930s were the American-born husband-and-wife team Marion Dorn (1899–1964) and Edward McKnight Kauffer (1890–1954). Their combined efforts in carpet and graphic design were among the most successful, and certainly flamboyant, expressions of Modernist Art Deco in Britain. In 1929 they exhibited their distinctive rugs at the Arthur Tooth & Sons Gallery in London. Made by the progressive manufacturer the Wilton Royal Carpet Company Ltd, in Wiltshire, England, the rugs demonstrated the change in taste towards Modernist interiors at the avant-garde end of the market. In a climate largely hostile towards the linear, unfussy and large field colouring of Modernism, Dorn, who specialized in furnishing textiles, created a unique look of her own (fig. 7). She used boxy, rectangular forms cut through by parallel lines that dynamically travelled across the surface of her rugs, which gave them simultaneously a sense of motion and a flattened architectural feel. Dorn's rugs, with delineated areas of plain colour, were usually in rich shades of brown and soft creams with the lines in contrasting shades. Her original white rug for the famous white drawing-room of 1933 of the decorator Syrie Maugham (1879–1955), a room remarkable for its use of white on white in an early emphasis on textures rather than colour, was the quintessential marker in avant-garde interior design at that moment. With its purity and suppression of colour and mixed texture, the version shown in fig. 8 (made in 1934 for a private apartment in Brighton, England) is very similar in essence, with a maze-like decoration formed by differing the height of the cut pile. Dorn's husband, McKnight Kauffer, came from an artistic graphic background, and in the late 1920s and early 1930s he created rug designs with

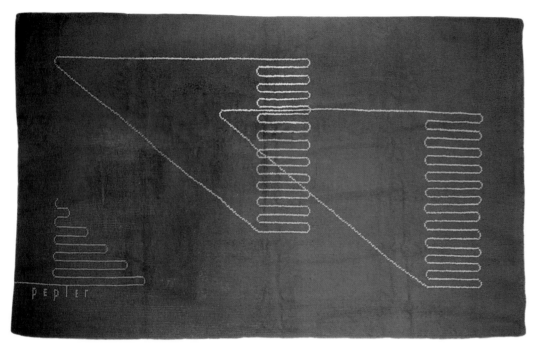

9. Marian Pepler, *Boomerang, c.* 1928–30, handknotted signed woollen-pile rug on a jute warp, probably produced by the Wilton Royal Carpet Factory Ltd, 203 x 325 cm (80 x 128.).

10. Edward McKnight Kauffer, 1929, handknotted signed wool rug produced by the Wilton Royal Carpet Factory Ltd, 258 x 258 cm (99 x 99 in.).

strong, boxy, abstract compositions with overlapping oblongs that juxtaposed bright colours. This handknotted signed rug of 1929 (fig. 10) was probably made at the Wilton Royal Carpet Factory, and belonged to Sir Francis and Dame Alix Meynell, whose house interior was decorated by Dorn in 1939; it is a comparatively tonally restrained example of McKnight Kauffer's style, with soft colouring but with the typical interesting placement of squares on the ground. The straight, clear lines that separated the colour fields in his rugs were often intentionally woven with bleeding edges in places, toning down the cutting sharpness of the forms. He liked to play around with his characteristic signature, 'EMCKK', which can be found woven in the pile in various forms on different rugs, and in this piece is simply 'EMK'.

More restrained and delicately and calmly composed than Dorn's or McKnight Kauffer's rug designs were those of Marian Pepler (1904–1997). Trained as an architect, in 1930 Pepler started designing rugs that were often intended to fit into overall interior schemes designed by her for the furniture and interior design firm Gordon Russell Ltd (frequently working with her husband, Richard D. Russell, the son of Gordon Russell). Her designs were greatly influenced by South American and other exotic decorative patterns, and incorporated ethnic motifs, which she often referred to in their titles – for example, *Peru* and *Puebla*.

She was also interested in representing different aspects of the earth's surfaces, as in *Beach* of 1933/34, made by Alexander Morton, and *Plough*, made by the Wilton Royal Carpet Factory in 1933, using natural colourings such as mushroom and brown. The chocolate-brown *Boomerang* rug, with "free line design in natural white on brown" (fig. 9), was handknotted at the Wilton Royal Carpet Factory in about 1928–30. This popular design was remade as a square version and was advertised in 1934 as part of a range of gun-tufted rugs designed by Pepler exclusively for Gordon Russell Ltd.[13]

Other avant-garde artists were invited to design rugs, and in 1936 the British Surrealist artist Paul Nash (1889–1946) designed two rugs for the architect Robert W. Symonds that were gun-tufted in Donegal.[14] Circular in shape, they were true to his Omega Workshops background, and in them abstract experiments in Cubism were fused with Fauve compositions that sprawled across the surface in a reduced palette of pale browns, taupes and greens. Although Nash had earlier lamented the slow process of handweaving rugs, he preferred the results of the true craft method to mechanical techniques.

Another artist, who was designing rugs before he became known for his painting, was Francis Bacon (1909–1992), who in 1929 had rugs made to his designs (fig. 11), and in 1930 displayed them, together with his own furniture, in his studio in London.

11. Francis Bacon, 1929, handknotted signed wool rug, possibly produced by the Wilton Royal Carpet Factory Ltd, 168 x 97 cm (66 x 38 in.).

12. Betty Joel, 1935–37, handknotted signed wool carpet produced in China, 269 x 180 cm (106 x 71 in.).

He attracted the attention of the contemporary design journal *The Studio*, which wrote: "His rugs are particularly representative of today and their inspiration springs from nothing oriental or traditional. They are purely thought forms … ."[15]

The softly coloured linear geometric-motif carpets by interior designer Betty Joel (1896–1985), with their sharply contrasting lines, required a finer finish and denser pile for a strong effect, and were handknotted in China. The example illustrated here (fig. 12) is also obviously influenced in its design by Far Eastern styles, as seen in the red circle, after the rising sun, and the Oriental calligraphic sweep of her initials in the pile. The lines around the motifs are also clipped in the pile, a typically Chinese technique, which gives a neater, finer result than is found in other modern carpets of the time.

Ashley Havinden (1903–1973) was another progressive British designer, who developed a distinctively British modern style that consisted of pale grounds with black, sweeping lines, often with graded shading on one edge, which swept across the rug in dynamic elegant motifs. He worked for J. Duncan Miller and the Wilton Royal Carpet Factory, for whom the *Orpheus* carpet (fig. 13) was designed; this was used in a J. Duncan Miller bedroom setting in 1937. Havinden often signed his carpets with just his first name in the weave, as can be seen in the design for the

13. Ashley Havinden, *Orpheus, c.* 1937, handknotted signed wool carpet produced by the Wilton Royal Carpet Factory Ltd for J. Duncan Miller, 318 x 234 cm (125 x 92 in.).

14. Ashley Havinden, design for *Orpheus, c.* 1937, body colour.

Orpheus (fig. 14). In the early 1930s he mixed with the Bauhaus émigrés in London and trained under the sculptor Henry Moore, who had a strong influence on his more progressive, asymmetrical, wavy designs.

The textile designer Ronald Grierson came relatively late to rug design, first developing an interest in this area in 1934. His early experiments in abstract compositions, as seen in his first one-man show in London in 1937, were highly influenced by the Cubist forms of Picasso and Braque. Grierson felt that a designer should be able to understand fully the technique and medium in which he or she was working and had a loom constructed so that he could weave his own rugs. His designs, catholic in nature for British tastes, were similar to those of Dorn and Havinden; most of them had plain backgrounds with simple but bold linear lines, and were classically balanced if a little bare. Grierson also had rugs woven by Jean Orage and some made in India, knotted in wool on a cotton warp to acquire a close pile, as well as producing designs for the Wilton Royal Carpet Factory, Tomkinsons and S.J. Stockwell.

The Silver Studio, which had been an influential London design studio since the late 1890s, was an important supplier of designs to the commercial rug market in Britain. Most of the designs by in-house designers were abstract patterns made less severe by the inclusion of sprigs here and there and the use of softened palettes of pale browns, with lurid oranges and greens. The more naturalistic aspects held greater appeal for the British popular taste in interior design at that time.

French progressive carpet design of the period 1910–39 can be broadly divided into three areas: traditional transitional, painterly colourist and Modernist architectural. Although boundaries were inevitably often blurred, all three areas come under the umbrella of Art Deco. Rug and carpet design in France was all about producing finely made, well-designed, unique works. The established carpet factories of Savonnerie, Aubusson, Cogolin and St Cyr gladly provided the weavers and production. The designers were plentiful and inspired, and were often well organized in the ateliers and firms of *décorateurs* and *ensembliers* in Paris and galleries such as the Galerie Myrbor of Marie Cuttoli (1879–1973), which was an important promoter of rugs and carpets by avant-garde artists.

Opportunities for designing rugs and interiors were broadening at this time; in addition to private work, there were important commissions to design complete interior schemes for shops, offices, banks and occasionally exhibition pavilions, and, most luxurious of all, the new ocean-going liners. The Exposition Internationale des Arts Décoratifs et Industriels Modernes held in Paris in 1925 allowed Europe to

15. Maurice Dufrêne, *c.* 1922, handknotted wool rug produced by Edouard Bénédictus, 122 cm (48 in.) diam.

show its achievements in the fine and applied arts. (The United States first exhibited at the 1937 Exposition.) The 1925 exhibition was particularly significant as the moment responsible for fusing many of the various design strands into what later became known as Art Deco. Because France was playing at home, its designers were all the more keen to be seen at their best and produced stunning carpets for their pavilions.

One of the most prominent interior-design studios was Süe & Mare, the partnership of Louis Süe (1875–1968) and André Mare (1887–1932). First formed in 1910 in the workshop of the Atelier Français, Süe & Mare produced traditional-transitional rugs. The compositions often contained period references and motifs such as garlands and shells, inspired by the Louis-Philippe style but with a contemporary slant. Mare had begun a painting career sharing a studio with the painter Fernand Léger and so had developed strong abstract Cubist tendencies. Süe & Mare's rugs, however, remained pretty, with flowered borders and patterned fields, although in forms more stylized than realistic. Süe, who had studied painting and architecture, had been influenced by German design. In 1918 they began working under the name Belle France, and a year later set up as interior designers in the firm Compagnie des Arts Français (CAF), for which they worked on the famous transatlantic liner

Ile de France in 1926. During this period they collaborated with figures such as André Derain, Raoul Dufy and Marie Laurencin, but in 1929 they more or less left decorating and returned to their earlier artistic and professional interests.

Another key style-setter was the Atelier Martine, set up in 1911 by Paul Poiret (1879–1944). Influenced by Poiret's contact with Josef Hoffmann at the Wiener Werkstätte in 1910, this was an extension of the French designer's Ecole Martine and was primarily an outlet for products designed and created by its female working-class students. Unlike the Viennese and German schools, however, the Atelier Martine provided its students with an alternative design education, encouraging them to extend their learning beyond traditional lessons to visiting alternative sources of inspiration such as zoos and botanical gardens. Sold through the Maison Martine, the rugs and other furniture and wares they produced were also greatly influenced by the avant-garde Cubist and Surrealist movements, in which the students were steeped. Their fresh, naïve motifs and colourful, loose, graphic style were extremely influential in Parisian interior design until the Atelier closed in 1934.

The *décorateurs* and *ensembliers* included Maurice Dufrêne (1876–1955), who, after 1921, was in charge of the workshop La Maîtrise at Galeries Lafayette. His Fauve-derived style was typified by densely

packed all-over vibrant floral patterns with stylized flowers in bright pinks and greens (fig. 15) that looked like huge, flattened bouquets or windows giving on to a garden in the centre of a floor. He was keen on unusual, round rugs, and showed a circular creation at the Salon d'Automne of 1931 in Paris. Also in this category was the *ensemblier* Emile-Jacques Ruhlmann (1879–1933), who had first shown rugs at the Salon d'Automne of 1911 but made more of an impact in the 1920s and 1930s. Working largely for the couturier Jacques Doucet, Ruhlmann had a very bold, modern style, often employing repeat motifs on richly coloured plain grounds, as in his circular rug for a reception room shown at the 1925 Paris Exposition. He also contributed to the decorations of the salons in the liner *Ile de France* in 1926.

Another significant Parisian atelier at this time was Pomone, which was established in 1922 at the Bon Marché department store and first run under the artistic directorship of Paul Follot and then, after 1932, René Prou (1889–1947). Follot had a pretty style, often using pastel colours and small, delicate flowers in decorative compositions. Prou was known as the first *goût moderne*, or 'modern taste', decorator, preferring a more simple, less ornamented style. Primavera, in the Au Printemps department store, was the other pace-setting decorating studio in Paris that was producing progressive

16. Fernand Léger, *c.* 1929, handknotted wool rug produced for Galerie Myrbor, Paris, 127 x 231 cm (50 x 91 in.).

carpets during this period. It was opened in 1913 by René Guilleré, who was one of the founding member of the Société des Artistes Décorateurs.

One of the most successful rug designers active in Paris at this time was Edouard Bénédictus (1878–1930), a Fauve artist and scientist. His designs were a mixture of light-coloured, geometric, Cubist forms, sometimes using stylized, sprig-like motifs taken from nature, with an orderly arrangement that was probably determined by his scientific mind. A much more avant-garde artist-designer was Sonia Delaunay (1885–1979). This Russian-born painter and designer created in her rugs syncopated, geometric shapes that were influenced by her involvement – along with her husband the painter Robert Delaunay – with set design for the theatre. The bright, solid colours of Diaghilev's Ballets Russes de Monte Carlo, for which they worked, were repeated in their rug designs. Pablo Picasso (1881–1973), one of the most renowned and versatile artists of the twentieth century, also worked with and was influenced by Diaghilev's ballet. During this period his rugs were patterned in a contained Cubist style, and, at the end of the 1920s, were made for Galerie Myrbor, along with those of Jean (Hans) Arp (1887–1966). Arp's designs were more abstract and anthropomorphic, with apparently randomly placed motifs on irregular square patches. The Cubist

artist Fernand Léger (1881–1955) created some striking abstract compositions for rugs, with stark, overlapping blocks, containing machine-like references, centred on a plain ground (fig. 16).

Other artist rug designers working in Paris included Henri Matisse (1869–1954) and Georges de Feure (1868–1928), a Dutch decorative artist who had Symbolist leanings and designed works in a heavy late Art Nouveau style. In contrast was the Polish-born Louis Marcoussis (1883–1941), who, designing for the studio of Jacques Doucet and for Myrbor, produced abstract, jagged, Cubist forms, probably influenced by the work of his friends Braque and Picasso. Valdemar Bobermann (1921–), an important and stylistically diverse rug designer, created designs using both abstract forms and naturalist motifs such as boats and human figures. In his well-known, painterly, linear composition of naked figures (fig. 17) there is a very naïve expression to the forms, which move around the ground to create a dynamic yet balanced pattern. Published in *Tapis Modernes* in 1929, it offered an interesting contrast to the largely unfigurative, abstract works that dominated French rug designing at this time.

The Leleu family of designers made a significant contribution to twentieth-century French rug design. Jules-Emile (1883–1961), who set up the company after World War I, was greatly influenced by

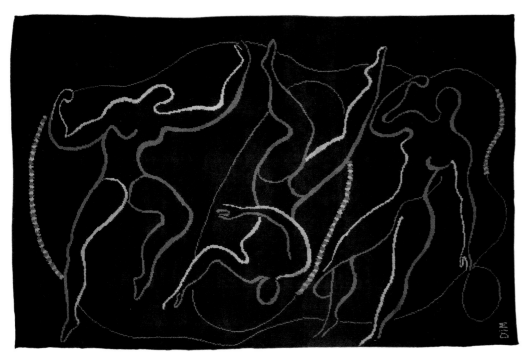

17. Valdemar Bobermann, *c.* 1929,
handknotted wool rug produced for
Décoration Intérieure Moderne,
300 x 194 cm (118 x 76 in.)

Ruhlmann and was later joined by his brother Marcel, daughter Paule and son André. Coming from an established family firm of painter-*décorateurs*, they first worked in the lavish, baroque style of the more traditional-looking rugs produced by the *ensembliers*. By the mid-1920s they had developed a more simple and distinctive form of Modernism, and exhibited at the 1925 Exposition. They were also involved in decorating many of the ocean liners that were so popular between the 1930s and 1960s, working on sections of the *Ile de France* in 1926 and using rugs by the master rug designer Ivan da Silva Bruhns, who was under contract to them, in the interiors of the *Atlantique*. Paule Leleu (1906–1987) trained under Da Silva Bruhns and, from 1932, designed the family firm's rugs for several decades.

Unlike most of his peers, Brazil-born Ivan da Silva Bruhns (1881–1980) was, after painting, solely concerned with rug designing. A master of the geometric composition, he is believed by some to be the finest of the rug designers in Paris at this time. He was inspired greatly by the Berber rugs and carpets he saw at the exhibitions of Moroccan art held in Paris in 1917 and 1918. Some of Da Silva Bruhns's most successful designs were for the commission of the Maharajah of Indore's palace of Manik Bagh, in India. In these he balanced linear geometric patterns with the striking colours adapted from North

African rugs, which resulted in stunning, richly coloured carpets (fig. 18).

Others who worked in a similar vein were Jean Lurçat, Robert Mallet-Stevens, René Herbst and the visitors to Paris, Eileen Gray and Evelyn Wyld. Jean Lurçat (1894–1970) was a pioneering architect in the Modernist vein, working in the style of the Bauhaus designer Marcel Breuer, and using searing colours in a monumental idiom drawn from Russian Constructivism, as seen in the carpets he showed at the 1925 Paris Exposition. In the late 1920s and early 1930s he designed some of the early Myrbor rugs, which were executed in Algeria for Marie Cuttoli. René Herbst (1891–1982), an architect and designer in the Functionalist camp, shunned ornament for plainer design statements, and was, in 1929, a founding member of the Union des Artistes Modernes (UAM).

Eileen Gray (1878–1976) was, like Da Silva Bruhns, interested in linear forms and compositions, and her rug designs were some of the most striking examples of the work of the French Modernist designers and were patterned with some of the most architecturally influenced forms. Her interest in both the new linear forms and the tactile and sensuous nature of the materials that surround us led Gray to create rugs that were intended to play an integral role within the designed architectural interior. The arrangements of geometric shapes in her early rugs of

around 1924, often abstract, interlocking squares, irregular stripes or large circles, were heavily influenced by the De Stijl art movement, with its flat, boxy elements in centralized groupings. They were often in contrasting colour fields with dark olive greens and mustard yellows, and her later black-and-white, circular rugs played with the curves of her occasional tables and seating. A self-taught architect who initially trained in lacquer work in London, Irish-born Gray moved to the more exciting artistic environment of Paris in 1902.

Another designer attracted to Paris from across the Channel was Evelyn Wyld (1882–1973). After working with Gray as manager of their weaving workshop, where Gray's designs were executed, she left in 1927 to design her own rugs and set up with the American Eyre 'Lise' de Lanux. Wyld had settled in Paris around 1907 and learnt weaving and wool-dyeing techniques in North Africa, on a trip with Eileen Gray. She also studied at the Wilton weaving workshops in England before setting up in Paris with Gray and then De Lanux. Working in a Modernist style, she was interested in stretching and dividing the rectangle shape of the rug with angular forms and breaking up areas with devices such as tufted elements. Wyld displayed her rugs at the second exhibition of the Société des Artistes Décorateurs in 1929, on a stand designed by and also showing the furniture of De Lanux. In 1937 she

18. Ivan da Silva Bruhns, c. 1930, handknotted wool rug produced at the Savigny manufactory in Savigny-sur-Orge for the palace of the Maharajah of Indore, 640 x 335 cm (252 x 132 in.).

was asked by the Metropolitan Museum of Art in New York to send one of her rugs to be represented in *Rugs and Carpets: An International Exhibition of Contemporary Industrial Art*, and provided one of her examples with a pale ground and strong, diagonal, dark lines and 'tufty' features. The following year she was requested to provide the same rug for the huge *Golden Gate International Exposition: A Pageant of the Pacific*, which took place in 1939 in San Francisco.

From 1927 to 1935 Eyre de Lanux made a number of rugs promoted by Wyld. Associating with avant-garde artists in Paris such as Henri Matisse, Picasso and Man Ray, she had a style that was a delicate adaptation of Cubist abstraction or near-realistic motifs, such as the naïve snail with its shadow published in *Tapis Modernes* in 1929.

The publication of M. Matet's *Tapis Modernes* was an important signifier that there was a substantial increase in the market for Modern rugs. Edited by H. Ernst, it contained more than eighty designs by twenty-five of the leading avant-garde rug designers in Paris. What is clear from this portfolio is that a synthesis of, on the one hand, traditional European and African folk motifs and, on the other, contemporary artistic movements and Modernist architectural motifs was taking place in French rugs. The results were startling, brash and innovative in the way that the ground of the rug was open to any combination of linear, geometric-abstract compositions with either brash colour fields or subtle, painterly shades. The traditional convention of border and field was almost forgotten. The designs had a vivacity and language of their own that related to the new artistic and architectural forms of Modernism and Art Deco, Fauvism, Cubism, Constructivism, Vorticism and Futurism, enveloping them at the same time as existing independently of them. These rugs were the paintings of the

applied arts and offered a bigger canvas and a different medium with which artists and designers could play.

In Austria the Wiener Werkstätte were producing young designers who were creating challenging carpets and rugs with soft, geometric, architecturally based repeat patterns. The established Professor Josef Hoffmann (1870–1956) was designing rugs for his architectural interiors, and these were executed by Joh. Backhausen & Söhne. The firm had also sent rugs to the important exhibition of rugs in New York in 1929, where works by Lois Resche and Philipp Hass were also shown as examples of contemporary Austrian carpet design.

One of the most important rug-weaving concerns outside France was the textile workshop of Germany's Bauhaus school of architecture, art and design, which operated between 1919 and 1933. Started by Walter Gropius in Weimar, it was a concerted attempt to bridge the gap between craft and industry in order to create commercially viable products that retained their artistic merit. Headed by Gunta Stölzl (1897–1983), the weavers were instructed in visual form theory, colour and design principles by the artists Paul Klee (1879–1940) and Wassily Kandinsky (1866–1944). These artists' characteristic compositions of surface planes made up of rows of squares in bright colours and different sizes, shapes and shades can be seen translated into the woven rugs and wall-hangings designed and woven by Bauhaus members such as Stölzl, Martha Erps (1902–1977), Annie Albers (1899–1994) and Gertrude Arndt (1903–2000). Stölzl was particularly interested in surface tensions created by the interplay of densely broken areas with larger, open grounds through the arrangement of rectangles of horizontal and vertical lines (fig. 19). The weaving workshops showed their works at the important Bauhaus exhibition *Haus am Horn (House at Home)* in 1923, where,

19. Gunta Stölzl, handknotted wool rug
produced in Turkey in 1998, in an edition
of 15, by Christopher Farr, London, from
a gouache design painted *c.* 1926,
360 x 250 cm (142 x 99 in.).

despite a lack of materials and the labour-intensive nature of the weaving (owing to the intricacy of the patterns, some rugs took three months to execute), the weaving workshops were, in terms of sales, the most successful Bauhaus discipline.

Also in Germany, Bruno Paul designed whole interior schemes, including rugs, and later received decorating commissions for ocean liners. After 1910 he developed a much tighter geometric style, creating rug patterns of smaller, detailed linear units, which were hand-made by the Vereinigte Smyrna-Teppich-Fabriken in Berlin in 1910. Among other rug and carpet designers who were working in a similar style in Germany after 1910 was A.E. Kopf. More florid were the designs of Richard Riemerschmid (1868–1957), who, in the opening years of the century, had been a great proponent of Art Nouveau. In 1910 his carpets were executed by the Deutsche Werkstätten für Handwerkskunst. In 1929 the works of Wilhelm Poetter, the textile designer Alen Müller and E. Andersen were sent to the New York exhibition of European rugs as representative of the best of contemporary German rug design. During the late 1920s and early 1930s a significant number of both hand- and machine-tufted rugs were being made in Germany for the English middle market. The work of less well-known designers, these tended to be of a mixed decorative style, with elements of Bauhaus-like Constructivism and naturalism combined in rather unstriking compositions with sober tonal effects. Compared with examples by Bauhaus or French designers, they appeared rather mediocre.

More radical forms of Art Deco found enthusiastic followers in both Western and Eastern Europe. The Dutch designer Jaap Gidding designed an eccentric carpet for the foyer of the Tuschinki Cinema, Amsterdam (1918–21). Czechoslovakia and Poland developed extreme elements, among which was the work of designers

20. Donald Deskey, *Singing Women*,
1932, wool carpeting for the Radio City
Music Hall auditorium, New York.

such as the Pole Stanislaw Brukalski. In
the mid-1930s he was working on ocean
liners, creating decorative forms that fused
traditional folk motifs with geometric lines
in the Moderne style, a luxurious form of
Modernism that veered towards Art Deco.

In Scandinavia the developments between
the 1910s and 1930s became known as
Scandinavian Modern. Characterized by
clean lines with pale colouring and fresh
patterns, the style was a combination of
traditional and rectilinear architectural
forms and the less lavish aspects of
international Modernism and Art Deco.
The *rya*, or *ryijy*, rug technique, which
produced a long and sometimes shaggy
pile, started to become more widely used
and anticipated its later popularity in the
1950s and 1960s.

One of the leading rug and textile
designers in Scandinavia at this time was
Märta Måås-Fjetterström (1873–1941). In
1919 she established an influential
workshop in Båstad that produced
handwoven rugs and carpets for a wide
range of progressive designers. Måås-
Fjetterström was fascinated by Persian
carpets and often incorporated, in a much
simpler form, the stylized flower motifs
that were common in Turkish carpets, but
placed them on softer pale grounds. Also
fascinated by traditional Eastern rugs,
Barbro Nilsson created progressive
patterns, playing with the richness of
colours but using more minimalist
compositions. More brightly coloured were
the Modern rugs of the Finnish designer
Impi Sotavalta (1885–1943). Her work in
the early 1930s, executed by Suomen
Käsityön Ystävät (Friends of Finnish
Handicraft), was strongly influenced by
the abstract-geometric pattern found in
the Bauhaus rugs of the late 1920s but
was woven in wool in a traditional low-pile
rya technique. Another Finnish-born
influential textile designer was Marianne
Strengell (1909–1998), who designed rugs

first in her native Helsinki and then, from 1930 to 1936, in Copenhagen, Denmark. Interested in the varying textures of the pile finish, she worked first for Hemflit-Kotiahkeruus and then for Bo Atieselskab. In 1937 she took her handweaving skills to the United States, where she settled and began teaching at Eliel and Eero Saarinen's Cranbrook Academy of Art in Michigan.[16]

Modern rugs had a limited profile in the United States until the spread from Europe of Art Deco in the early 1930s. As immigrants with strong national traditions of flatweave indigenous rug design and hooked-rug techniques, many leading designers of woollen-pile rugs brought the influences of their native art and culture to their adopted country. Contemporary rugs and carpets had not, however, been completely ignored in the United States. Carpets were featured in the 1926 Metropolitan Museum of Art's exhibition of objects from the hugely successful 1925 Paris Exposition, which had not included American products. The second exhibition of European applied arts, organized by the Division of Industrial Arts of the American Federation of Arts in New York in 1929, was a significant event in the world of rug designers as it showed contemporary rugs from Europe.[17] Bringing new ideas to the American public and designing fraternity, the exhibition included rugs by those designers considered to be the best representatives of progressive rug design in France, Germany, Sweden, England, Austria and Belgium.

Already working in a Modernist idiom at this time was the designer Donald Deskey (1894–1989). Having spent time training in Paris in the 1920s, he was one of the first to experiment with abstract-geometric patterns in the United States. One of that country's most striking and bold rug designers, Deskey was responsible for overseeing the interior decoration of the

new and dynamic Radio City Music Hall in 1932, for which he designed the carpeting in the main auditorium (fig. 20). This was a unique opportunity for Art Deco designers, and the notable textile designer Ruth Reeves (1892–1966) designed the foyer carpeting. This was highly influenced by her earlier training under Fernand Léger in Paris and mixed French Cubist with jazz-modern decoration in what were to become the established dominant colours of American Art Deco: brown, orange and cream. Also working in abstracted designs in the United States at this time was the Frenchman Jules Bouy (1872–1937). Essentially a metalwork designer, he had had an interior-design business in Belgium until he crossed the Atlantic in 1913. In the early 1930s he designed a number of wall-hangings and rugs, including a striking tree-patterned chenille bath mat with strong colouring. An emigrant from Budapest, Hungary, in the same year was Ilonka Karasz (1896–1981), who was followed in 1914 by her sister Mariska Karasz (1898–1960), who also worked in textile design. Ilonka often drew on Eastern European traditional folk art for the figurative elements of her rugs, which were composed in the brown tones and manner of early Art Deco. The style of another European settler in the United States was largely informed by her native Finland; Loja Saarinen (1879–1968) continued to design rugs in the 1930s, and was responsible for making them for other designers such as Frank Lloyd Wright, and her husband, Eliel Saarinen (1873–1950), at the Cranbrook Academy of Art. In the early 1930s the Austrian Pola Hoffmann, who had been trained in architecture at the Kunstgewerbeschule in Vienna, was also designing rugs. Eugene Schoen (1880–1957), another important rug designer in New York, mainly designed abstract rugs for one-off commissions, but also created triptych pieces in the form of

broken-up sunbursts. In nearby Maine during this period, John A. Storrs was designing and making hooked rugs to progressive patterns.

By the late 1930s the atmosphere was ripe for an exhibition dedicated to rugs and carpets, and in 1937 New York's two major contemporary-design exhibition venues both held shows. The Museum of Modern Art held an exhibition of *Rugs from the Crawford Shops Designed by American Artists*; they specialized in hooked rugs made by traditional methods but to contemporary designs. Many of the same artists also appeared in the Metropolitan Museum of Art exhibition of rugs and carpets held in the same year. Such was the importance of the French examples shown that in 1939 the Metropolitan Museum of Art acquired a number of rugs from the Myrbor Galerie in Paris.

21. Unknown British designer, *c.* 1940, handknotted wool rug produced by the Savonnerie manufactory, 633 x 384 cm (249 x 151 in.).

The 1940s and 1950s in Europe saw the design excesses of the 1930s wane as a result of World War II. Between 1939 and 1945 many designers were either involved in the war effort or found that their markets had disappeared. In 1940 Marion Dorn and Edward McKnight Kauffer were forced by their need for employment to leave London and return to the United States, where he set up in practice as a graphic artist in New York and she tried to establish herself again as a rug and interior designer. Although Dorn managed to rebuild a certain amount of her British reputation, she never quite re-created the standing she had enjoyed in Britain. Betty Joel closed down her carpet business during the war years, while Ronald Grierson continued to design and weave his rugs on his own loom but had a limited market.

There was in Britain, however, a mid-range market for toned-down, less brightly coloured and flamboyantly patterned linear late-Art Deco rugs. The more symmetrical and paler tones were much more suited to the conservative British taste and often depicted starburst-like patterns radiating out from the centre of the ground (fig. 21). In Britain the market increased for commercial, machine-woven contemporary-patterned rugs. Companies such as T.F. Firth & Sons Ltd in Brighouse, Yorkshire, produced Scandinavian-derived long-pile *rya* rugs, made on an Axminster Jacquard Gripper, and, in addition to the more conservative Finnish and Swedish designs, they produced some brightly coloured, almost lurid, contemporary patterns. Quayle & Tranter Ltd of Kidderminster, Worcestershire, who placed the highest emphasis on the quality of colouring and design, also produced their Q Norsk range of *rya* rugs, designed by known figures such as Peter McGowan and Fay Hillier. The company had the largest representation of carpets chosen by the independent selection committee at the important *Britain Can Make It* exhibition held at the Victoria and Albert Museum, London, in 1946, which was the first post-war opportunity for British companies to display their most up-to-date products. Other firms, such as Wessex Weavers in Wilton, Salisbury, and the Chlidema Carpet Co. Ltd of Kidderminster, were also influenced by handmade rug designs from the 1930s in their rug collections of the 1940s and 1950s. During this period the abstract artist Graham Sutherland (1903–1980) and the Modernist architect-designer Raymond McGrath (1903–1977) were, ironically, commissioned to carry out much more traditionally based designs for broadloom carpets for hotels and university buildings.

Conversely, in the United States in the 1940s there was a more adventurous picture. Commercial, artistic and curatorial interested parties were actively promoting handmade contemporary-designed rugs. After the success of the 1937 exhibitions in New York, the Metropolitan Museum of Art held an exhibition in 1941 of *Rugs by Modern Artists*. Largely supported by the print artist Ralph M. Pearson (who had recently opened his own weaving workshop), this featured 'imported' works by the cream of the late-Art Deco rug designers working in France, including Fernand Léger, Louis Marcoussis, Joan Miró and Jean (Hans) Arp. It inspired artists and manufacturers in the United States to create their own unique and contemporary rugs. This resulted in another exhibition a year later of *New Rugs by American Artists*, which showed works by ten American artists, including what was probably the last rug design by McKnight Kauffer, as well as the abstract, pattern-orientated *Flying Carpet*, designed by Stuart Davis (1894–1964) and gun-tufted with cut-loop pile of wool yarn on jute canvas by V'Soske of Grand Rapids, Michigan.[18] This firm made all the pieces

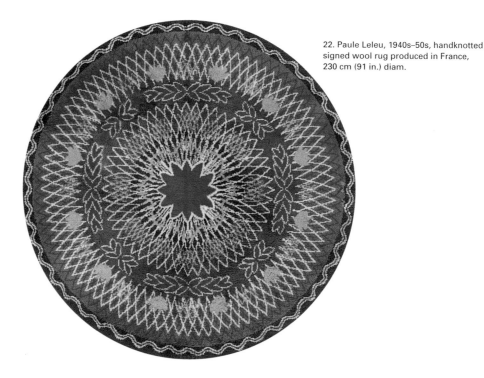

22. Paule Leleu, 1940s–50s, handknotted
signed wool rug produced in France,
230 cm (91 in.) diam.

for this exhibition, including a handknotted, jellyfish-like patterned carpet by John Ferren that was subsequently acquired by the Museum of Modern Art. The show, retitled *Rugs by American Artists*, then toured the United States and Canada for the following two years. V'Soske was also making gun-tufted rugs in unusual places such as Puerto Rico for designers including Frank Lloyd Wright. In 1951 Wright designed for his son David Wright a carpet that was heavily influenced by the overlapping circular compositions of scientific-related patterns, which were a long way from his restrained linear expressions of the beginning of the century.

The general surge in interest in Scandinavian design in the late 1940s and the 1950s was no less marked in the field of rugs. Although designers and weavers continued to be true to traditional Scandinavian weaving techniques and styles and even to Eastern carpet patterns, the simple, subtle designs and well-made results were highly influential across Europe and the United States. The growing popularity of the traditional *rya* long-pile technique, for example, led to an increasing preference for textural qualities and tactility over pattern. By the late 1950s and the beginning of the 1960s it was widely used as a way of creating depth and as an alternative expression of the surface pile. Scandinavian designers found a welcome interest, particularly in the United States,

and the Finnish-born textile designer Marianne Strengell developed modern versions of *rya* rugs with bright colours and striped patterns. This growth in interest was behind the exhibition *Design in Scandinavia*, which travelled across the United States from 1954 to 1957.

In France many artists and designers continued to practise throughout the 1940s despite the rationing of materials. Many of the rugs and textiles produced challenged the lack of dyes and resulted in much more interesting compositions that relied on interaction of patterns rather than colour. Paule Leleu developed busy patterns with arrangements of geometric motifs such as baton-like shapes arranged in circles. She also continued to produce designs that became much more influenced by the patterns derived from science and technology that were being incorporated into the decorative arts in the 1940s and 1950s. She experimented with 'spirograph' waves running around circular rugs and simplified floral motifs, often with grounds in toned-down earthy colours (fig. 22). Such work encapsulated the energy of the post-war optimism and was typical of the interest shown by designers in new, unhistorical and non-naturalistic decoration. Other *décorateurs*, such as Louis Süe, continued with their historically derived patterns, but in a much more minimalist and subtle form, and the result was a somewhat architectural style, not

dissimilar in feel from the works of André Arbus (1903–1969) of this time.

The Galerie La Demeure in Paris (1950–81) was successful in raising the profile of new, artist-designed carpets. Many of its pieces were made in Marrakesh until Morocco gained independence in 1956, as well as at the long-established Manufacture Française de Tapis et Couvertures in Beauvais, which opened a workshop for handknotted carpets in 1943. The Atelier Primavera (at the Au Printemps department store) was very active in the 1950s, as was Emile Gilioli with his abstract compositions. Lucienne Coutaud was designing for Gobelins/Mobilier National in the 1950s, and Jean Picart le Doux was creating striking modern compositions with motifs in dynamic arrangements. Other less decorative and more artistic and abstract expressions were being designed by the American-born Alexander Calder (1898–1976) for Marie Cuttoli at the Galerie Lucie Weill in Paris, and by the Swiss-born Paul Klee (1879–1914), the Frenchman Fernand Léger (1881–1955) and the Spaniard Joan Miró (1893–1983). *La Mangouste* (fig. 23), originally designed for Marie Cuttoli at Galerie Myrbor but re-executed at the Galerie Lucie Weill in the 1940s or 1950s, is representative of Miró's disparate compositions of surreal, extruded, biomorphic forms, which both he and Calder were also renowned for in their paintings. In The Netherlands in the 1950s,

23. Joan Miró, *La Mangouste*, c. 1941, handknotted signed wool rug produced by the Savonnerie manufactory, rewoven 1960s/1970s, 153 x 207 cm (60 x 81 in.).

24. Märta Måås-Fjetterström Workshop, c. 1941, handknotted wool rug, initialled in pile 'ABMMF', 335 x 230 cm (132 x 91 in.).

rugs and carpets of a tame, abstract-geometric decorative style were being designed by Elsbeth Fehmers and C. Koevoet for Koninklijke Vereenigde Tapijtfabrieken NV of Moordrecht.

In Sweden the weaving workshop in Båstad, AB Märta Måås-Fjetterström, was still operating and producing rugs and carpets by a range of designers. Up until her last year the works of Märta Måås-Fjetterström (1873–1941) retained their calm, orderly feel, often with stylized flower motifs, taken from Eastern designs, in soft, pastel colours on a pale ground (fig. 24). In 1943 the workshop was producing rugs with dark grounds and elliptical forms scattered in groupings across the field, as found in Turkish carpets. An example is *The Shells röllakan* carpet of Barbro Nilsson (who was artistic director, after the death of the firm's founder, from 1942 to 1971), where the Swedish forms are more stylized and the composition has a looser, sporadic feel. In the 1940s Föreningen Svensk Hemslöjd (set up by Kristianstad Lans Hemslojd) was producing *rya* rugs with simple patterns of basic motifs.

Similar products were coming out of Norway, such as those made at the State School for Women's Crafts, with bare, stick-like designs on pale grounds. More contemporary designs were also experimented with, such as the circular, gun-tufted pile rug designed by Ulrikke

Falck-Jorgensen and woven by Anna Tørresdal in natural-coloured sheep's wool with earthy dyes. The pattern of two bands of radiating darts pointing inwards towards the centre, which is brighter than the rest of the rug, was typical of the period in its use of graduating shades. Design influences worked both ways, and a design for a rectangular, gun-tufted pile carpet by Anne Lise Kndtzon has similarities to the line arrangements of squared motifs of Paule Leleu, who was working in France at this time. A more extraordinary pile carpet, designed by Kjellaug Hølaas and woven by Sigrin Berg for the Norwegian Employers' Association around 1952, had an abstract-geometric composition, with a contorted set of squares containing motifs all set at a slant across the surface.

During the 1950s the Finn Uhra-Beata Simberg-Ehrström (1914–1979) was gaining international recognition with her carefully composed and subtly coloured *rya* rugs. These were striking in their use of a controlled palette that was sophisticated in its placing of muted shades and tones in simple, geometric patterns, which allowed the surface texture to become prominent. In Denmark Gerda Henning (1891–1951), who was designing and weaving her own pieces at the same time as teaching weaving, also produced simple, modern designs. Some of these she handwove herself, and she sold other designs for manufacture by L.F. Fogth in about 1949/50.

1960s–1970s: Pop, Op and Fun

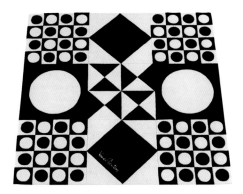

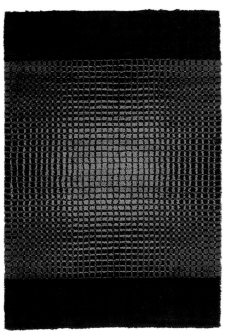

25. Verner Panton, *VP IV*, 2001, after
Geometry IV carpeting 1959/60,
gun-tufted wool carpet with relief-cut
pile produced by Teppiche Drechsle KG,
Germany, 210 x 210 cm (83 x 83 in.).

26. Gaetano Pesce, *Kyoto*, mid-1970s,
looped-pile wool rug produced in Italy,
244 x 168 cm (96 x 66 in.).

27. (opposite, detail) Heal & Son Ltd,
Pop Art Rug, mid-1960s, looped-pile
wool rug, 198 x 137 cm (78 x 54 in.).

"Art takes on a new perspective when translated into inventive modern rugs that can be spread on floors … ."[19]

The 1960s and 1970s saw a resurgence in the importance of the role of the rug in highly designed interiors that was closely linked with the artistic movements of those decades, which ranged from Abstract Expressionism in the United States to the Pop Art and subsequent Op Art styles, the last of which was particularly popular with Italian designers. As in the 1920s and 1930s, artists were engaged to create designs for rugs, carpets and carpeting, and this raised the whole profile of handwoven flooring. Rug design during these decades was seen as a reaction against the minimalism and restraint in the surface pattern of Modernism. This was coupled with a continuing interest in the more traditional aspects of the materials and the techniques of handicrafts. The period was also significant for the 'globalization' of design style, whereby, more than ever before, the ideas of artists, designers and architects were converging into a world look that could be found from Europe to the United States, from Japan to Brazil. This era saw the re-emergence of the professional designer as a high-profile figure in a creative industry. Originating in the 1930s, this trend had been stemmed by World War II and had taken over a decade to regain momentum.

The reaction against the largely austere colours and restrained patterns of the 1940s and 1950s resulted in an explosion of colour, particularly in Abstract Expressionism and Pop Art and in the striking, geometric compositions of Op Art, which explored the various optical effects achieved by retinal stimulation. The progressive London manufacturer and retailer Heal & Son Ltd produced rugs with striking compositions in bright colours (fig. 27). Challenging and fun, the arrangements of overlapping circles with linear forms broke up the field and created a play of tonal recession with the different shades of colour. The designer who took this to its most extreme forms was the Danish-born Verner Panton (1926–1998), who created optically challenging, co-ordinated complete interior schemes. The early 1960s saw the culmination of his 'Geometry' series, with *Geometry I* winning the 1963 International Design Award AID in the United States. *Geometry IV* was wall-to-wall carpeting in which the repeat pattern of circles and squares of various sizes was made exciting with the stark, contrasting extremes of black and white (fig. 25). Another designer interested in the possibilities of Op Art and woven wool was the American-based Florence Knoll-Bassett (born 1917). Her black-and-white pin-striped rug had a similar aesthetic to Panton's works and also echoed Op Art paintings of the time by artists such as Bridget Riley.

Italian designers who were turning their interests to rugs included Gio Ponti (1891–1979) and Gaetano Pesce (born 1939). Pesce's play with weave, pile and Op Art pattern was extraordinary. His long-tufted rug (fig. 26) of the mid-1970s is a stunning example. Carefully placed, graduating lines of squares in three shades of brown that change tonally across the surface create a visually convincing illusion of an artificially lit shimmering metallic surface. Pesce was formerly a kinetic film-maker, and his interest in creating moving images is seen here as he subtly plays with the effects of the extra length of the pile to suggest a sense of movement in a static object. More interested in the acid swirls of psychedelic colouring was Sandra Marcantonato, who was designing and weaving handknotted rugs in Italy in the late 1970s.

Also interested in the surface texture qualities of rugs were designers such as the Finnish textile and rug designer Uhra Simberg-Ehrström (1914–1979), who was

28. Pablo Picasso, *Jacqueline, c.* 1969, handknotted wool rug produced in France, 175 x 226 cm (69 x 89 in.).

known as the "inventor of the *colour ryijy*".[20] In her *Sprout* rug, designed in 1973 and woven by Pirkko Sillfors in 1979, she explored the subtle nuances of different shades and, through different weave techniques, brought attention to the plasticity of the pile surface. Her fellow countrywomen Ritva Puotila (born 1935) and Kirsti Rantanen (born 1930) were more interested in the contrasts of textures within a rug's surface. In Rantanen's 1979 *Blanket of Snow*, which she designed and wove in the same year, the long, white *rya* pile with slits of flatweave *raanu* hint at something hidden below a layer of white snow.[21] Hilkka Vuorinen (born 1924) was interested in the possibilities of contrasting black and white to create a sense of surface tension and movement. This was achieved in her dynamic *In the Sea* of 1965, woven in 1975 by Anneli Hartikainen of the Friends of Finnish Handicraft, which suggested the play of natural light on white foam above a

deep, dark ocean. More fashionable was the work of Ib Antoni for Egetaepper of Denmark, whose *rya* rugs of 1973/74 were decorated with psychedelic, atom-bomb cloud forms in purples, blues and browns.

Generally, after the vivid and intense colours of the 1960s, designers of the 1970s were interested in experimenting with colour in a much more subtle fashion. British designers such as Ronald Grierson (see p. 22) were heavily influenced by rugs based on craft techniques rather than by the more artistic patterned designs. Experimenting with different surface textures, many rug designers working in Britain in the 1960s used Scandinavian-influenced *rya*, tufted and flatweave kilim techniques; among these were Klares Lewes, Helen Hutton and Brian Knight. They also included textile designer Marianne Straube, who experimented with striped long-pile rugs, creating surfaces with a ribbed look, as well as working

29. Ellsworth Kelly, *Primary Tapestry*, 1967–68, handknotted wool rug from a planned edition of 20 of which approximately 4 were made, for the Charles E. Slatkin Gallery, New York, 304.5 x 302 cm (120 x 119 in.).

with contemporary trends in contrasting black-and-white patterns. Across the Channel the *Actualité et tradition du tapis* exhibition in 1963, organized by the Galerie La Demeure in Paris, was successful in raising the profile of new, artist-designed carpets in France.

In the United States a series of exhibitions aimed to revive the handwoven rug and carpet industry, historical and contemporary. In 1962 the World House Galleries in New York held an exhibition of twenty-six rugs mixing the work of past Modern masters such as Léger, Miró and Picasso with that of the contemporary designer Miriam Leefe. Her abstract works were remarkable for their interest in textural surface. Also committed to bringing together past and present was an exhibition of woven rugs and hangings called *American Tapestries*, which established weavings as a cogent link between art and decorative design. Held in 1968 at the

Charles E. Slatkin Galleries, New York, it showed works after paintings by twenty-two Pop Art and Abstract Expressionist artists, who were very much involved with the designing of the rugs, which were woven in India. Their interests in the expression of surface equated with the qualities of the handknotted wool or silk pile. The event's success led, in 1970, to a second commercial exhibition of artist-designed rugs, *Modern Master Tapestries*, which was important as a benchmark and suggests that there must have already been a growing interest in pile weaving, as well as a need to promote it. The term 'tapestries' seems to have been used interchangeably for a floor covering or a wall-hanging, and this says something about contemporary attitudes towards the woven rug, which could live happily in either realm. The exhibition also included works by both past masters, such as Léger and Picasso (fig. 28), and contemporary

30. Roy Lichtenstein, *Modern Tapestry*, 1979, handknotted wool rug produced in India, in an edition of 20, for the Charles E. Slatkin Gallery, New York, 274 x 368 cm (108 x 145 in.).

31. Andy Warhol, *Marilyn*, c. 1966, handknotted signed wool rug on a cotton warp, probably produced in India, from a planned edition of 20 of which about 4 were made for the Charles E. Slatkin Gallery, New York, 183 x 183 cm (72 x 72 in.).

32. Jack Lenor Larsen, *Fantasy,* 1980,
wool carpeting woven on a Wilton loom
with worsted yarns in four colours and
tweeds of two or more colours.

American painters, in an attempt, as stated in the catalogue, "to give new expression to an ancient form".[22] New twists were given to existing works by established artists such as Robert Indiana. His now iconic 'Love' motif, already painted, printed and sculpted, was, in 1967, given a new dimension in a woven, handknotted, all-silk pile rug and retitled *Lovewall*. Ellsworth Kelly's *Primary Tapestry* creates an interesting architectural relationship, with the acute angle of the rug pattern echoing the corners of the room (fig. 29). The Pop Art 'anti-sensibility' dynamic compositions of Roy Lichtenstein (born 1923), which include loud, busy, striking motifs from modern life, were given a less severe form in a handknotted wool version made in 1979. The woven lines of *Modern Tapestry* (fig. 30), made in an edition of twenty, softens the commercial coolness and precision of the painted work. The icon of them all, Andy Warhol's *Marilyn* (fig. 31), was

reinterpreted as a handknotted wool weaving of about 1966, of which only about four were made. The uneven edges of the woven, curvaceous lines complement the equally blurred definition of the original screenprint and painting.

The American Crafts Council Museum of Contemporary Crafts (ACCMCC) also held shows of rugs and carpets, often exhibiting experiments in new types of material such as in the retrospective exhibition of 1970 for rug designer Dorothy Wright Liebes (1897–1972), which included gun-tufted prototypes in DuPont nylon, as well as her more artistic *Firebird* single-needle-tufted wool rug of 1960. The ACCMCC's *Contemplation Environs* exhibition of 1969 had included rugs with more unusual uses, and Urban Jupena's *Dimensional* woven rug of that year was intended to fill a whole room and act as a lounger as well as a floor covering, reflecting the lifestyle concerns of the period.

At this time one of the major protagonists of textile and rug development and promotion at the top end of the market in the United States was Jack Lenor Larsen (born 1927), who, in 1980, was the subject of a retrospective exhibition at the Musée des Arts Décoratifs at the Louvre in Paris. Larson was concerned with both the commercial and the aesthetic aspects of rugs and carpeting. His *Fantasy* rug, launched in 1980, was directly inspired by nature, rather than artistic or design movements (fig. 32). Later developed as carpeting, the design was based on a motif taken from a traditional Tibetan rug, while the colouring was inspired by a visual and aesthetic experience Larsen had had while glancing up through the leaves of a Norwegian maple tree. Noticing that the red and green colours were of equal intensity, he attempted to repeat this in a textile rug, showing that nature can successfully inform art and craft.

1980s –2001: Post-modernism, Faith, Craft and a Brave New World

33. Ettore Sottsass, early 1980s, gun-tufted wool rug produced by Tisca, France, 230 x 180 cm (91 x 71 in.).

34. (opposite, detail) Jody Harrow, *Rocks at Ise*, 1990, gun-tufted wool rug produced by Tisca, France, 275 x 180 cm (108 x 71 in.).

The 1980s witnessed a huge expansion in the market for one-off and multiple-edition handmade rugs and carpets as well as for designer- and artist-designed carpeting. Both interest and production continued to grow strongly throughout the 1990s, and by the beginning of the twenty-first century the profile of rugs and carpets, as both important components in interior design and works of artistic merit, had been raised significantly, so that they enjoyed a heightened presence in many interiors. This was partly due to the rise in popular interest in interior design. A positive economic climate and the growing fashion for loft-living in converted warehouses led many people to choose well-designed, good-quality furnishings. The decorative style most often adopted for such homes was Neo-modernist purity, with its characteristic white walls and uninterrupted pale-wood floors. People soon realized, however, particularly in the colder climates of Northern Europe and the East Coast of the United States, that, for both practical and decorative reasons, the broad expanses of wood-strip floors needed to be made less stark. Beautifully designed and well-made woven rugs were the perfect solution.

The other main factor contributing to the growth of the field was the active promotion of handmade rugs and carpets by enlightened designers, studios and retailers. One slightly negative aspect of the boom in demand for artistically designed rugs is the increase in gun-tufting, which does not result in as fine a quality as the finish produced by handknotting. While it is undoubtedly crucial for the more commercial, contract end of the market, the technique limits the possibilities of the design and compromises designers.

From the mid-1980s a small number of designers and manufacturers were promoting handmade rugs and carpets. Christine Van Der Hurd, in London and New York, and, in London, Christopher Farr

and Helen Yardley of A–Z Studios were experimenting and developing designs, production techniques and markets. In both the USA and Europe V'Soske was, as it had been doing for many decades, actively commissioning and producing progressive rugs. In Germany the firm Vorwerk started experimenting with its carpeting range by inviting designs from well-known avant-garde artists.

At this time the design impetus came from three main areas. One source was traditional Eastern and European carpet patterns; another was the desire for a purely artistic expression, including the more architectural style of Post-modernism; and the third was the aim to meet the needs of a decorative approach to interior design.

The Italian Post-modernist design studio Memphis and the American architects Michael Graves (born 1934) and Robert Venturi (born 1925) had dramatic influences on rug and carpet design during this period. The American version of Post-modernism was more rooted in architecture. Using architecturally derived references and motifs that were then deployed in unusual decorative contexts, it had a playful character, and rugs were a perfect medium for this expression. Michael Graves's *Rug No. 2*, designed, signed and dated in pile in 1980, and gun-tufted in 1984, was one of three rugs that V'Soske commissioned him to design. The surface of the rug is used like a stage for the enactment of an architectural drama. Like figures in a Greek tragedy, the scattered fragments of what could be a cornice moulding cry out from the corner. The remaining ground is harmonious, and, although made up of different elements that are asymmetrically scattered, the composition maintains a certain order and balance in its use of earthy colours and decorative forms.

For the international Memphis design group, based in Milan, all-over surface

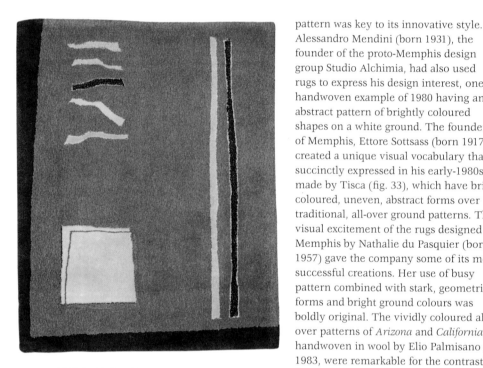

35. Helen Yardley, *No. 34*, c. 1985, gun-tufted wool rug produced in England, 167 x 127 cm (66 x 50 in.).

pattern was key to its innovative style. Alessandro Mendini (born 1931), the founder of the proto-Memphis design group Studio Alchimia, had also used rugs to express his design interest, one handwoven example of 1980 having an abstract pattern of brightly coloured shapes on a white ground. The founder of Memphis, Ettore Sottsass (born 1917), created a unique visual vocabulary that is succinctly expressed in his early-1980s rugs made by Tisca (fig. 33), which have brightly coloured, uneven, abstract forms over traditional, all-over ground patterns. The visual excitement of the rugs designed for Memphis by Nathalie du Pasquier (born 1957) gave the company some of its most successful creations. Her use of busy pattern combined with stark, geometric forms and bright ground colours was boldly original. The vividly coloured all-over patterns of *Arizona* and *California*, handwoven in wool by Elio Palmisano in 1983, were remarkable for the contrasting forms that are thrown together in an apparently organized disarray on a plain, light ground, and were exhibited in *Ten Modern Carpets* in the United States for Palmisano. The playful form of E.B. Jackson's rug for Memphis (available at the time through Dennis Miller Associates) followed the shape of the water splash it was depicting, and this idea was an important Memphis design statement. The *Oregon* rug by Gerard Taylor (born 1957) was much more restrained than any other Memphis flooring, but its strong, varying coloured lines, very Modernist in construction, relate to some of the profiles of Memphis furniture. Nathalie du Pasquier and George J. Sowden (born 1942) also designed carpeting for the English company Steeles Carpets Ltd, which made its *Calculus* design as an 80% wool, 20% nylon contract-grade carpeting. This carpeting, patterned with compactly detailed, ziggurat-stepped, wiggle-like

motifs, created the illusion that the surface of the floor was reeling and thrashing about. A sense of movement could also be found in the rugs of Charles Vandenhove (born 1927), who, in 1992, designed a series of gun-tufted carpets in which the ground was covered in repeated architectural forms resembling rows of windows in a high-rise block, with *trompe-l'œil* shading. Jo Crepain (born 1950) also designed a gun-tufted rug with an Op Art-type pattern of thin bars flying out of space in a vortex. William Morris would have strongly disapproved of three-dimensional pattern underfoot, but this was the essence of Post-modernism – the use of unexpected decorative patterns in what were traditionally inappropriate ways to challenge the perception of design.

Also promoting unusual carpeting, which contributed to the general promotion of woven flooring during the 1980s, Vorwerk launched an artist-designed range that continues to be developed in the new century. This collection included a huge list of international artists and architects such as Roy Lichtenstein (born 1923), Sol LeWitt (born 1928), Jeff Koons (born 1955), David Hockney (born 1937) and Zaha Hadid (born 1950). The designs removed all existing barriers regarding what were appropriate patterns for the floor, and created striking atmospheres that transformed internal environments. Outstanding examples are Hockney's wriggly, maggot-like, repeated squiggles, Jeff Koons's meadows of summer flowers, Lichtenstein's stripes and spots that stretch out across the floor, and the spine-chilling, thin trails of blood that flow across the white ground in pieces by Sam Francis (1923–1994).

Christine Van Der Hurd (born 1951), a British textile designer first active in New York, has been designing and producing rugs since 1981, most of which have been made in Nepal. As a maker of custom floorings, she was particularly concerned with the effects of the colours of rugs in

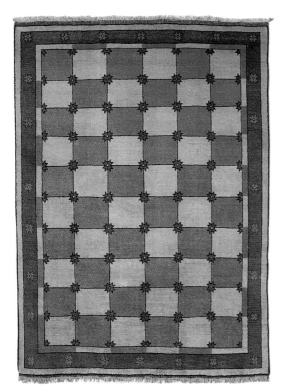

36. Christopher Farr, *Untitled*, 1987, handknotted wool rug, 200 × 150 cm (79 × 59 in.).

interiors and created well-balanced, geometric patterns, which resulted in rugs and carpets that were intended for interiors of contemporary design. Operating in a more painterly vein, Helen Yardley (born 1954) designed carpets that were, and still are, delicate balances of colour harmony and composition (fig. 35). The irregularly profiled forms had a certain naturalness and calmness, recalling the tranquillity of Far Eastern art. The use of grey with black, white and a dash of bright red was a very typical interior colour scheme of the mid-1980s.

Christopher Farr (born 1953) and Matthew Bourne (born 1960) have successfully promoted good-quality, well-designed rugs and carpets since their company was established in London in 1991. A trained painter, Farr started by designing his own rugs in 1984; these were often contemporary interpretations of traditional Turkish rugs (fig. 36), with brighter, cleaner colours and clearer, boldly defined motifs. After his successful exhibition *Brave New Rugs* at the Royal College of Art, London, in 1991, the studio has inspirationally commissioned many well-known carpet and textile designers, including Kate Blee (born 1961), Georgina von Etzdorf (born 1955) and Allegra Hicks (born 1961), as well as the couture fashion designers Romeo Gigli (born 1949) and Rifat Ozbek (born 1953), who brought their unique statements to rug art and design, and whose pieces are handknotted or flatwoven in Turkey. From the mid-1990s the company was working with avant-garde fine artists and product designers such as Michael Sodeau (born 1969), Michael Young (born 1966), Tony Bevan (born 1951), Sarah Morris (born 1967), Gillian Ayres (born 1930), Gary Hume (born 1962) and Gavin Turk (born 1967), the last of these using the surface of the woven pile as a form of canvas, extending the boundaries and shared territory of the weaver and the

artist. Farr was also responsible for remaking classic designs from original artwork, such as the Bauhaus carpets of Gunta Stölzl (fig. 19), in the best possible quality and replicating the original colouring as closely as possible; these were shown in a well-received exhibition at the gallery of the Royal Institute of British Architects, London, in 2000.

Also reworking classic designs, Emilio Pucci (1914–1992) in New York reproduced a dynamic 1960s design in 1984 (fig. 37). This was signed in the pile four times, and the energetic mix of dynamic composition with pastel shades and grey is typical of the mid-1980s use of colour and form. More recently, in 2001 the German company Teppich Drechsle launched the Verner Panton Carpet Collection. Working with Panton's widow, it has developed a striking range of carpets, derived from his carpeting and textile patterns of the late 1950s and 1960s, that capture the essence of Panton's Op Art-psychedelic trademark (fig. 25).

More traditional craft-based one-off rugs were being designed and woven by Stella Benjamin (born 1933), on her American-Indian Navajo loom in Cornwall, England, and by the established British designer-weaver Peter Collingwood (born 1922). Other craft-based one-off carpets designed in Britain were shown in the travelling exhibition *Six Chairs and Six Rugs* in 1992, which featured striking contemporary pieces by the high-profile designers Jennie Moncur (born 1961), Helen Yardley (born 1954), Sandie Ennis, Fiona Nealon, Jason Collingwood (born 1963) and Sally Hampson (born 1954). The last two used more unorthodox combinations of weaving materials such as horsehair, linen and raffia, which, by 2001, was an increasingly popular practice, particularly with carpets woven in Tibet and Nepal. The Washington, D.C.-based company Cloud IX, which makes rugs in the Himalayas, has specialized in producing carpets with

37. Emilio Pucci, *c.* 1980, gun-tufted signed wool rug produced in Italy in an edition of 12, based on a 1960s design, 228 x 152 cm (90 x 60 in.).

contemporary designs inspired by patterns from the earth's surface and woven in Tibet in mixed natural fibres including wool, silk and allo (a material derived from the Himalayan Elephant Nettle). A British-based company also utilizing the skills of Himalayan weavers is Veedon Fleece. Established in 1992, it has a diverse range of contemporary and traditionally derived rugs, and is unusual in that it has no retail outlets, preferring to remain more exclusive for its clients. Also less influenced by Western fine-art and high-design traditions are the Eastern-orientated works produced by Dudley and Madeleine Edwards of Amazed, based in Yorkshire, England. With patterns made of carved piles depicting mazes and crop circles, the carpets are woven in wool, jute and hemp, and are intended to compliment the peace-invoking lifestyle and interiors.

In the mid-1990s a more purely artistic exercise was initiated by the Belgian Atelier Vermeersch in Ghent, which promoted the integration of the rug as a craft object with its role as a work of artistic expression. Commissioning eleven German and eleven Belgian artists, the firm produced a highly expressive body of rugs in which the line between art and craft was obliterated; these were exhibited in Ghent in 1995 and Berlin in 1996. A similar venture was the *Woven in Oaxaca* exhibition, held in 1997 at the A/D gallery, New York, where artists were commissioned to design rugs that were woven in hand-carded and hand-dyed wool in editions of six (fig. 38). The results were extremely individualistic, as is the rug-focused work of American artist Chuck Close (born 1940). His translation of a portrait into a rug in *Lucas Rug* (1993) is a breathtaking exercise, combining abstract colour to build up a slightly obscure but intricately detailed picture using each carefully placed knotted thread of silk (see p. 80). A challenging contribution to contemporary rug and carpet design

has also been brought by the Japanese designer Shiro Kuramata (born 1934), who exhibits a palpable delight in American popular culture.

The year 2001 saw more handmade rug and carpet collections launched across Europe and the United States than ever before. Their presence has highlighted the interesting diversity of rug styles and quality available at the beginning of the twenty-first century. With stunningly designed carpets handknotted in silk by the Fort Street Studio (see pp. 86–89) and the more Eastern-inspired and executed examples from Odegard and Michaelian & Kohlberg, all of New York, it is good to know that the art and quality of rug- and carpet-making are still high on the agenda. From a more unusual perspective, the works in the 'Groundplans' collection of Jody Harrow-Le Guillou, also of New York, are exercises in hyperrealism – all-over compositions accurately reproducing flowers, pebbles and leaves in three dimensions (fig. 34). Gun-tufted in France, they overturn William Morris's beliefs that only flat pattern was suitable for a floor carpet. Aimed at the more contemporary interior-design market are the Verduno area rugs, which are designed to co-ordinate with the firm's interior furnishings range of textiles, and the pleasing and fun geometric designs of Angela Adams, of Maine, in the United States, which are gun-tufted in that country.

Among the more commercial of the contemporary rug producers are the German company Bärbel and Wolf Bruns, whose striking geometric carpets are gun-tufted in various parts of Europe and the East, and, in France, Toulemonde Bochart, which has commissioned various top designers, including Andrée Putman, Hilton McConnico and Helen Yardley. London has the recently established Loopy, making funky-patterned gun-tufted rugs, as well as the more serene, painterly designs

38. *Woven in Oaxaca* exhibition at the A/D gallery, New York, 1997. Each of the rugs was made in an edition of 6, and employed hand-carded and (where dyes were used) hand-dyed wool.

of Baris Chochan (born 1971). Also in London, Little + Collins, one of the longer-established companies producing handmade carpets, has created sophisticated, striped linear compositions on its handmade pieces, with subtle shades of contrasting soft colour, often with shearing to create different planes. The brightly coloured striped and abstract gun-tufted designs of the Brazilian Chichi Cavalcanti (born 1965) are a fresh appearance on the London rug scene. With a now well-established and exciting stable of top designers, the Christopher Farr studio in London is creating an environment that challenges designers to push back both the technical and the design boundaries of handmade rugs. The studio commissions designers such as Kate Blee, whose 'Flood' collection (see p. 72), exhibited at the Pucci Gallery in New York in May 2001, challenges, like the carpets from the Fort Street Studio, the boundaries between technical skill, craft and art.

Another British company that has been exploring the possibilities of artist- and designer-designed rugs is Kappa Lambda, which in the past few years has brought out progressive collections by, among others, the British architect Nigel Coates (born 1949), the Franco-Italian partnership Garouste (born 1949) and Bonetti (born 1953), Kate Blee and Susan Absolon. The trend for designers to work internationally can be seen in the 2001 collection of the Swedish design company Asplund. Its 2001 range includes carpets designed by the Britons Michael Sodeau (born 1969) and Tom Dixon (born 1959), the Australian-born Marc Newson, the Italian Stefano Giovannoni (born 1959) and the Swedish architect Thomas Sandell (born 1959).

At the end of the twentieth and beginning of the twenty-first centuries the expectation that rugs and carpets should be merely floor coverings has been seriously challenged. As in the 1960s, lifestyle changes have influenced how we use the furnishings around us. In this climate designers such as Michael Sodeau have created woven carpets such as *Blue Rug* for Christopher Farr, which doubles as a lounger and carpet, and as such is part of the late twentieth-century design trend for alternative, multi-functional flexible furniture (see pp. 46–47, 166).[23]

At the start of the new century the possibilities for handmade rugs and carpets have reached an exciting high point. As globalization brings about the synergy of different centuries-old skills and traditions with contemporary design, the challenge for designers and producers is to combine the quality offered by handweaving techniques with designs that maximize the beauty of the medium, with sensitivity and style.

Susan Absolon

Disco
Gun-tufted wool, 1996
Produced by Kappa Lambda, London, UK
274 × 183 cm (108 × 72 in.)
Courtesy of Kappa Lambda, London, UK

This rug is typical of the work of Susan Absolon, in which
strong, vibrant colours are used within amorphous shapes to
produce an overall pattern. In this case the ovoid shapes
around the edge form a border, while the shapes held within
the panel in the middle act as a central motif.

Susan Absolon

Loose Talk
Gun-tufted wool, 1996
Produced by Kappa Lambda, London, UK
245 cm (96 in.) diam.
Courtesy of Kappa Lambda, London, UK

In this design the brave use of two tones of powerful blue
makes a very strong statement. Close inspection reveals that
the design is made up of various letters and punctuation
marks. These work well within the format of a circle, as the
design 'reads' from whichever direction it is approached.

Angela Adams (born 1965)

Manfred
Gun-tufted wool, 1999
Produced by Angela Adams, Maine, USA
213 × 213 cm (84 × 84 in.)
Courtesy of Angela Adams, Maine, USA

The rounded corners and organic shapes in this rug owe
a good deal to the revival of 1960s and 1970s design that
occurred from the mid-1990s, exemplified by home furnishing
publications such as *Wallpaper** magazine. Indeed, in years to
come, many people may place this design in that earlier period.

Angela Adams

Grace
Gun-tufted wool, 2000
Produced by Angela Adams, Maine, USA
213 × 213 cm (84 × 84 in.)
Courtesy of Angela Adams, Maine, USA

The very small scale of this pattern calls for great skill
in execution and would be extremely hard to achieve with
any technique other than gun-tufting. The manner in
which the design gravitates towards the top corner is highly
original, and this, combined with the use of two soft
colours, makes for a sophisticated design that, although
busy, is also easy on the eye.

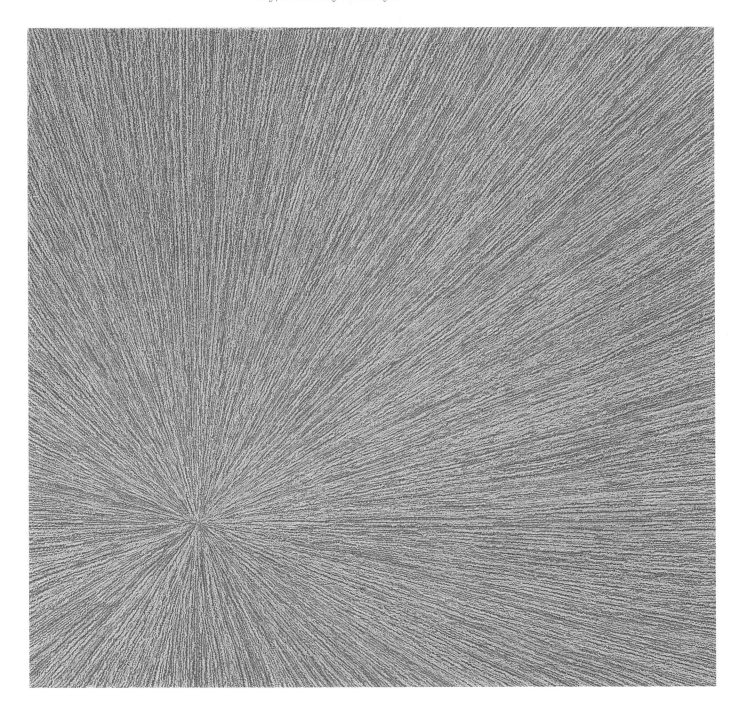

Gillian Ayres (born 1930)

Sithond's Snows
Handknotted wool, 1998
Produced by Christopher Farr, London, UK
Based on the artist's painting *Sithond's Snows*, 1990
Edition of 15
245 cm (96 in.) diam.
Private collection, France

It is always worth questioning the premise of an artist basing
a rug on a painting, as opposed to designing a piece specifically
for the medium. But in this case the image was so inviting and
suggestive of the handknotting process that a rug made after
the painting was attempted. The process of translation creates
another object – equally beautiful but different. In the artist's
view the rug contains the essence of the original inspiration,
which came from Rajasthan, India.

Chris Baisa (born 1964)

Passage
Handknotted wool, 1999
Produced by Elson & Co., San Francisco, USA
244 × 300 cm (96 × 108 in.)
Courtesy of Elson & Co., San Francisco, USA

This piece has a very simple format that somehow has
a marked 1990s feel to it. The centralized design, gravitating
towards the hot orange in the middle, would have implications
for the rug's use in a furnishing scheme, and the work
is probably intended as a centrepiece for a room.

Cressida Bell (born 1959)

Untitled
Handknotted wool, 1993
Produced by Christopher Farr, London, UK
Edition of 10
280 × 185 cm (110 × 73 in.)
Private collection, UK

Bell was inspired by the rare garden carpets of sixteenth-century Persia, which represent the next world awaiting the pious, and has successfully incorporated this influence into her own work. The design is notable for its fourteen borders, leading to a central rectangle depicting water, and for its stylized fish.

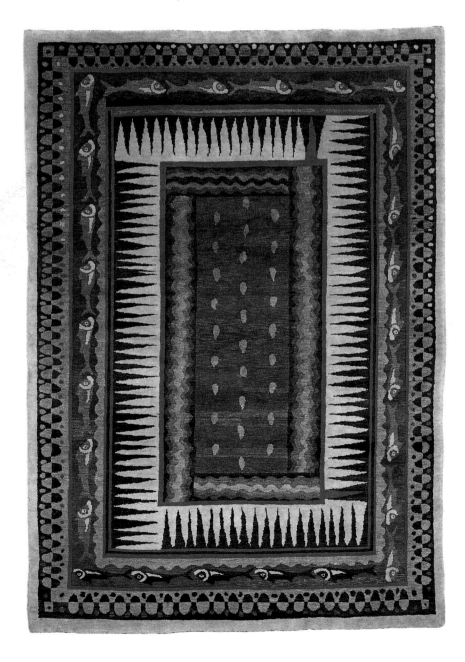

Cressida Bell

Wheels
Handknotted wool, 1994
Produced by Christopher Farr, London, UK
Edition of 10
241 × 150 cm (95 × 59 in.)
Private collection, London, UK

A stunningly detailed and well-thought-out work such as this one absorbs the more obvious conventions of rug design while not compromising the designer's own vision. Although at first glance it seems that Bell pays little regard to the style of her celebrated Bloomsbury forebears, there is nevertheless an unmistakable affinity.

Stella Benjamin (born 1933)

Yellow Rug
Handwoven flatweave, Navajo technique, wool, 1999
Woven by Stella Benjamin
218 × 203 cm (86 × 80 in.)
Private collection, UK

Stella Benjamin is unique in the sense that she weaves all
her own work and designs it on the loom. Rather than using
any artwork or pre-drafted design, she holds the motifs and
patterns in her mind, much like a weaver from the nomadic
tribes of southern Iran such as the Quashgai. As the loom
Benjamin works on is narrow, wider pieces such as this one
are made in two parts and then sewn together. The vibrant
yellow in this piece was hand-dyed by Benjamin herself
on to handspun yarn.

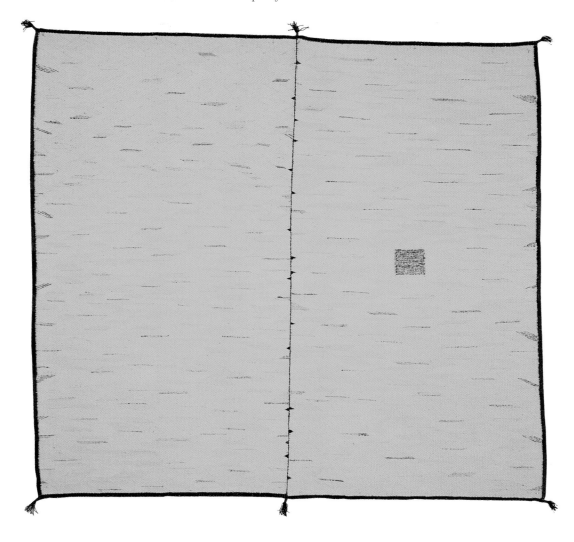

Stella Benjamin

Red Rug
Handwoven flatweave, Navajo technique, wool, 2000
Woven by Stella Benjamin
193 × 304 cm (76 × 120 in.)
Collection of Chester Jones, London, UK

The use of intricate 'lazy lines' in this piece breaks up the red
ground into many different zones, and the careful selection of
yarn tells us that this is no random effect, as it can be in other
flatweaves. Benjamin is extremely concerned with controlling
the movement of colour in the field to meet her exact
requirements, much as a painter would with a brush.

Tony Bevan (born 1951)

Rafters
Handknotted wool, 2001
Produced by Christopher Farr, London, UK
Based on the artist's painting *Rafters*, 1999
Edition of 10
220 × 150 cm (87 × 59 in.)
Courtesy of Christopher Farr, London, UK

The journey from the paint and charcoal of the original painting, to hand-dyed wool and a weaver's hand tying thousands of individual Turkish knots on to vertical warps, is an exacting process, worth pursuing only if the artist can find a new way of expressing his or her original intent. This rug succeeds in expanding the artist's primary practice in an additional medium.

Tony Bevan

Rafters
Handknotted wool, 2001
Produced by Christopher Farr, London, UK
Based on the artist's painting *Rafters*, 1999
Edition of 10
358 × 280 cm (141 × 110 in.)
Courtesy of Christopher Farr, London, UK

This rug plays interesting games with our perception.
Designed by artist Tony Bevan, it will spend its life on a
floor, looked down upon by children and adults alike, who
may well be wondering a little as to the origins of the design.
They are in fact contemplating a rug made from a painting
about what it is like to look up into the partially destroyed
roof of an old building.

Kate Blee (born 1961)

Sun
Handknotted wool, 1992
Produced by Christopher Farr, London, UK
Edition of 10
196 × 178 cm (77 × 70 in.)
Private collection, London, UK

There is something endearing about the way in which
a weaver relates to a design that was created far from his
or her immediate environment. Here there is an exciting
tension between the weaver's tentative, shaky line and
the designer's sophisticated intention. Modern British and
American painting is never far from Kate Blee's thinking, yet
her use of colour in this rug is strikingly unusual and fresh.

Kate Blee

Untitled
Handknotted wool, 1993
Produced by Christopher Farr, London, UK
Edition of 10
213 × 213 cm (84 × 84 in.)
Collection of Anthony Hyde, London, UK

These two rugs by Kate Blee illustrate two contrasting styles.
The earlier design, below, is from the geometric period of her
career as a rug designer, while the runner opposite shows
a switch to a more organic, 'all-over' approach.

Kate Blee

Field
Handknotted wool, 1993
Produced by Christopher Farr, London, UK
Edition of 10
275 × 75 cm (108 × 30 in.)
Private collection, New York, USA

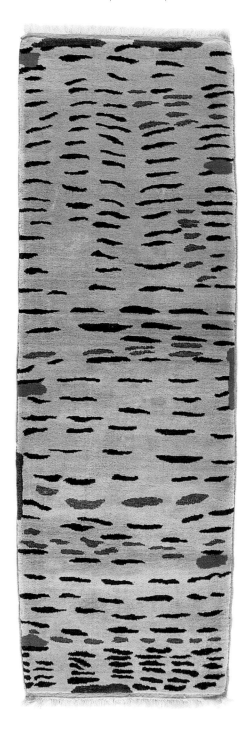

Kate Blee

Circle
Handknotted wool, 1993
Produced by Christopher Farr, London, UK
Edition of 15
244 × 183 cm (96 × 72 in.)
Private collection, London, UK

The rug has often been used in the West to mark out space.
It is frequently placed in the hearth area of the living-room,
banked by opposing sofas or chairs to help emphasize an area
where people meet. Here Kate Blee has designed a circle
within a rectangle to reinforce the idea that a rug can be the
focal point of a room.

Kate Blee

Herringbone
Handknotted with handwoven flatweave border, wool, 1993
Produced by Christopher Farr, London, UK
Edition of 10
277 × 74 cm (108 × 29 in.)
Private collection, Hong Kong, China

The separation of abstract shapes from any connection with natural forms has rarely been achieved. Here the pattern evokes dry-stone walls, or the well-known jacquard weave. The intense indigo dye, which repeatedly saturates the high-lustre handspun wool and mohair, gives the design a depth of colour any painter would envy.

Kate Blee

Tiger Kilim
Handwoven flatweave, wool, 1994
Produced by Christopher Farr, London, UK
Edition of 25
245 × 180 cm (96 × 71 in.)
Private collection, New York, USA

Unusually for Blee, this flatweave has a border containing a field of amorphous forms that can be reproduced by the flatweave technique with a high degree of accuracy and sensitivity as they are all tending towards the horizontal. However, the vertical black lines at top and bottom are not so successful, owing to the amount of interlocking required where the two colours meet.

Kate Blee

Bar 1 + 2
Handwoven flatweave, wool, 1998
Produced by Christopher Farr, London, UK
Edition of 10
Both 274 × 80 cm (108 × 31 in.)
Private collection, London, UK

These two flatweaves are part of a larger series of same-size runners to be used in conjunction with one another. It is also possible to butt the separate pieces together to form a larger flatweave. Here fun is to be had, as the placement of the pieces can be changed at will to make a new design. Other colourways can be added to broaden the modular possibilities.

Kate Blee

Block
Handknotted wool, 1998
Produced by Christopher Farr, London, UK
Edition of 15
275 × 183 cm (108 × 72 in.)
Private collection, Rio de Janeiro, Brazil

Designing with just two colours, Blee has created three
separate areas by building up layers of lines that appear to
be randomly uneven. In fact it requires more attention from
the cartoon-maker and the weaver to produce this rug correctly
than would be needed if the lines were straight or had any
symmetry. Close inspection reveals no repetition in this design.

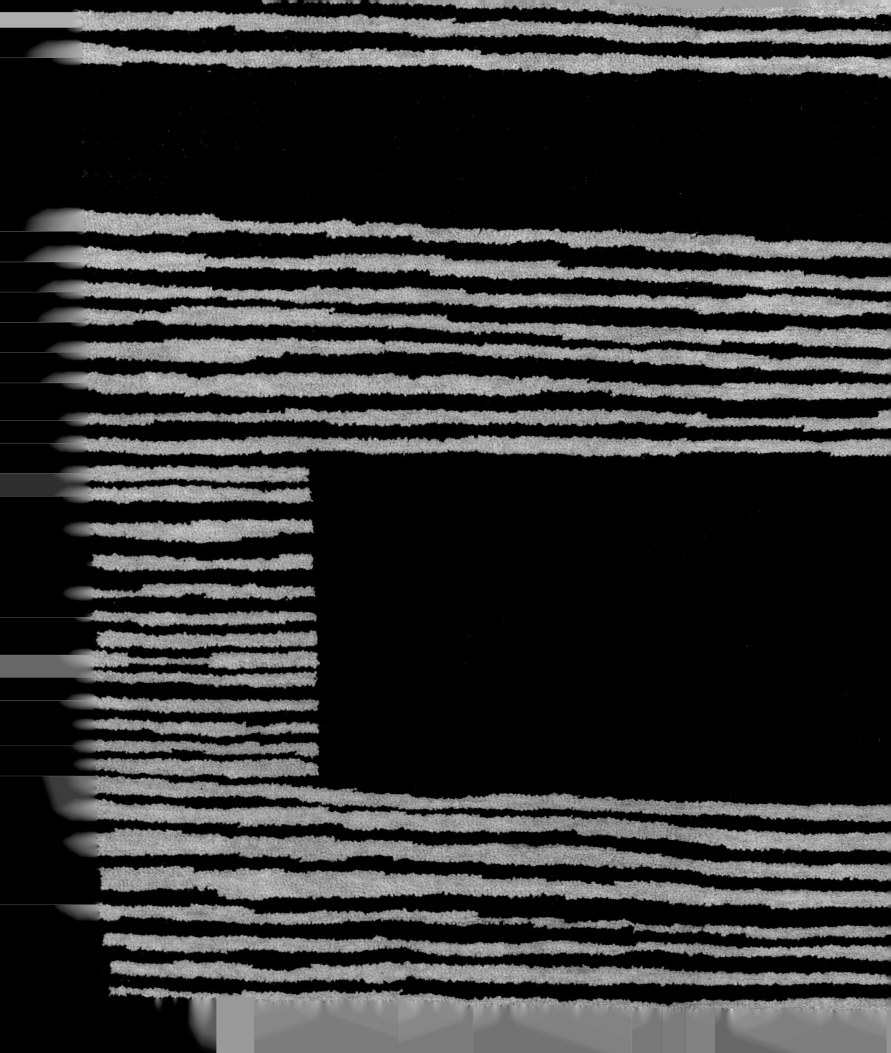

Kate Blee

Heat
Handwoven flatweave, wool, 1998
Produced by Christopher Farr, London, UK
Edition of 15
200 × 150 cm (79 × 59 in.)
Private collection, London, UK

This flatweave shows the designer's understanding of how
a traditional Turkish weaver works. What at first glance
appears to be a sophisticated minimalist design reveals,
on closer inspection, a structure of trapezoid shapes that fill
up carefully proportioned colour fields.

Kate Blee

Left Hand
Handwoven flatweave, wool, 1998
Produced by Christopher Farr, London, UK
Edition of 15
275 × 183 cm (108 × 72 in.)
Courtesy of Christopher Farr, London, UK

Blee based this flatweave on a freehand drawing that was made using only her left hand – hence the title. The meandering, horizontal white line is the perfect device for the technique, as the weaver has little difficulty in reproducing the irregularities of the original drawing accurately and crisply.

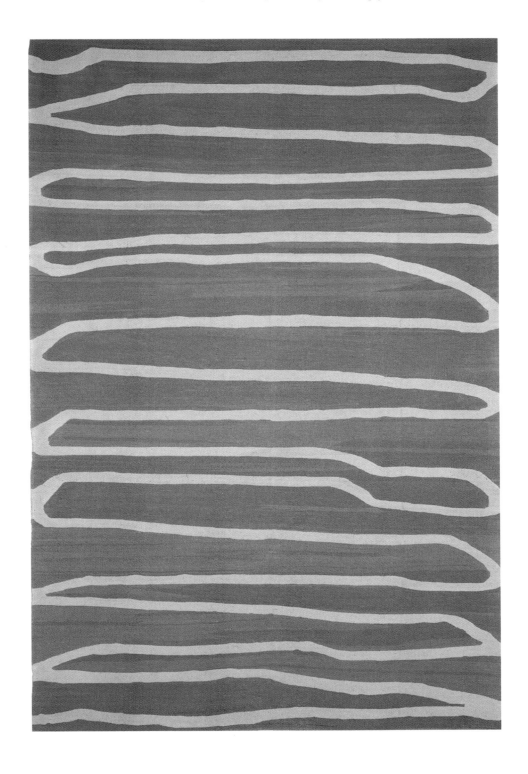

Kate Blee

Cast
Handknotted wool, 2001
Produced by Christopher Farr, London, UK
Edition of 15
305 × 245 cm (120 × 96 in.)
Courtesy of Christopher Farr, London, UK

In the late 1990s Kate Blee visited her parents' remote home
in south-east France to witness at first hand the devastation
caused by the worst floods for a hundred years. The drawings
that resulted from this visit have been translated into a series
of rugs entitled 'Flood'. Rock fall on the area's scree slopes
inspired this work, which suggests the new shapes revealed
as slate blocks sheered away from the rock face.

Kate Blee

Chalk
Handknotted wool, 2001
Produced by Christopher Farr, London, UK
Edition of 15
305 × 245 cm (120 × 96 in.)
Courtesy of Christopher Farr, London, UK

This rug, with its intense luminosity, demands to be placed
centre stage. It is the type of rug that warns off any furniture,
insisting that it be admired alone for its arresting beauty.

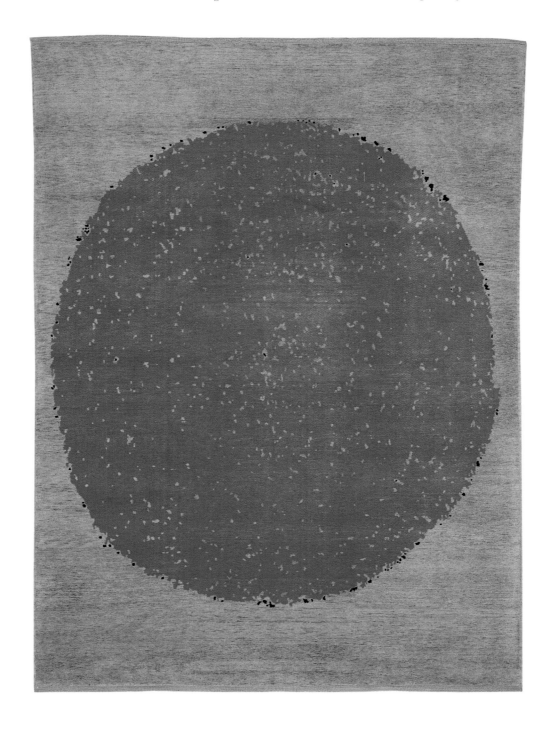

Barbara Bloom (born 1951)

Lolita
Gun-tufted wool, 1999
Produced by Peter Blum, New York, USA
Edition of 15
213 × 152 cm (84 × 60 in.)
Courtesy of Peter Blum, New York, USA

Artists have traditionally employed any number of subtle devices to reach us. A numb, jaded audience needs to be teased a little to create space for it to receive a new impression. This delightful rug takes an iconic subject and playfully places it beneath our feet, bringing to the surface a rich haul of thoughts, images and memories.

VLADIMIR NABOKOV

LOLITA

Volume Two

THE
OLYMPIA

Alighiero Boetti (1940–1994)

Alternating One to One Hundred and Vice Versa
Handwoven flatweave, wool, 1993
Edition of 50
287 × 272 cm (113 × 107 in.)
Courtesy of Gagosian Gallery, New York, USA

"At P.S1 [Gallery, New York] were shown [the then recently deceased artist's] final spectacular series of kilims, that transformed the space into a kind of contemporary mosque. The carpets sang of times both ancient and modern, and they implicitly addressed the terrible and inexcusable ruptures that exist between the east and the west and the so-called third world. They are an assertion of folk traditions that still just survive in the east, and equally of the domination of the new digital communication technologies that threaten to become the basis of our new virtualized culture. We cannot make the latter go away but, unless we become conscious of its negative possibilities, it will surely eliminate those beautiful, ancient techniques based on the handloom. For it is subtleties allowed by the handloom, the warp and the weft that permit the particular complexities of the pattern that has given the carpet and the tapestry its potent richness and symbolic complexity throughout history. Not for nothing were carpets and fabric hangings more highly prized in Europe by princes and those who collected objects of value, than the most exalted painting."
(Courtesy of Norman Rosenthal, *Recognizing Alighiero Boetti*, 2001, Gagosian Gallery, New York, USA)

Sharon Bowles (born 1962)
& Edgard Linares (born 1960)

Reverso
Handknotted wool, 1997
Produced by Christopher Farr, London, UK
Edition of 10
250 × 180 cm (98 × 71 in.)
Courtesy of Christopher Farr, London, UK

These amorphous shapes have a sculptural quality rare in contemporary rugs. Balance and directed eye movement seem paramount to these designers, whose choice of industrial materials is counterpointed by an almost fragile sensitivity. An important consideration for any designer is the rug's relationship to its immediate surroundings. In this case, placing a table or a chair on the rug will change everything.

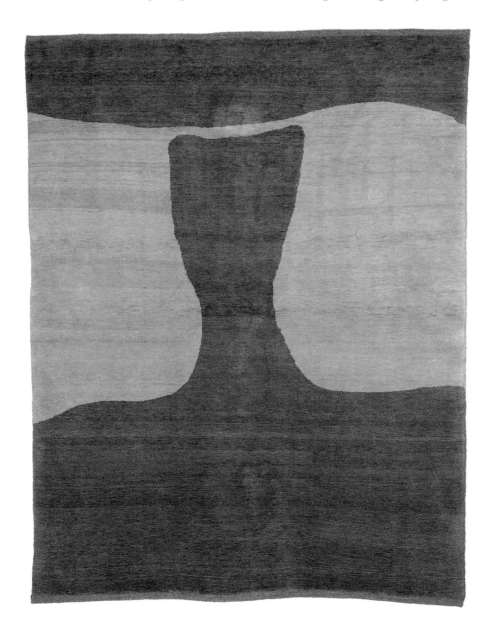

Sarah Cheyne (born 1964)

Untitled
Handknotted wool, 1993
Produced by Christopher Farr, London, UK
Edition of 10
245 × 180 cm (96 × 71 in.)
Collection of Christopher Farr, London, UK

Sarah Cheyne was one of the textile students who took part
in the groundbreaking exhibition *Brave New Rugs* at the
Royal College of Art, London, in 1991. This design started out
as a collage, and the handweaving process has managed to
retain that spirit.

Chuck Close (born 1940)

Lucas Rug
Handknotted silk, 1993
Produced by A/D, New York, USA
Edition of 20
201 × 168 cm (79 × 66 in.)
Courtesy of A/D, New York, USA

Step back two paces from this rug by Chuck Close and you
can see the whole face. The closer you are to the surface, the
more diffuse and abstracted the image becomes. This is an
exquisitely crafted rug from a unique artist, whose paintings
of heads have taken portraiture into hitherto unknown realms.
It is constructed in a manner not dissimilar from pointillism:
thousands of knots form clusters of circles within circles,
which, together with the precise use of dark and light tones,
make up the whole head.

Nigel Coates (born 1949)

Big Square
Gun-tufted wool, 1998
Produced by Kappa Lambda, London, UK
200 × 200 cm (79 × 79 in.)
Courtesy of Kappa Lambda, London, UK

The renowned London-based architect Nigel Coates produced
the 'Oyster' collection of which this design is a part. The
design is based on one simple motif that rotates and repeats
in the middle. This centralized interest makes the rug one
that would draw the eye wherever it was placed in a room.

Vincent Dane (born 1949)

Circle Line
Handwoven flatweave, wool, 2000
Produced by Robert Stephenson, London, UK
381 × 252 cm (150 × 99 in.)
Courtesy of Robert Stephenson, London, UK

Robert Stephenson, an established dealer of antique Oriental carpets in London, has, like others, recently turned to new production as the supply of old pieces reaches exhaustion. He commissioned artist Vincent Dane to design a group of flatweaves that he has had woven in Romania, in the area formerly known as Bessarabia, where highly decorative 'Oriental' flatweaves were produced in the decorative European floral style during the nineteenth century and the beginning of the twentieth century. It is apparent from this updated version of such work, and from the example overleaf, that the weavers of this area are very comfortable working in this way.

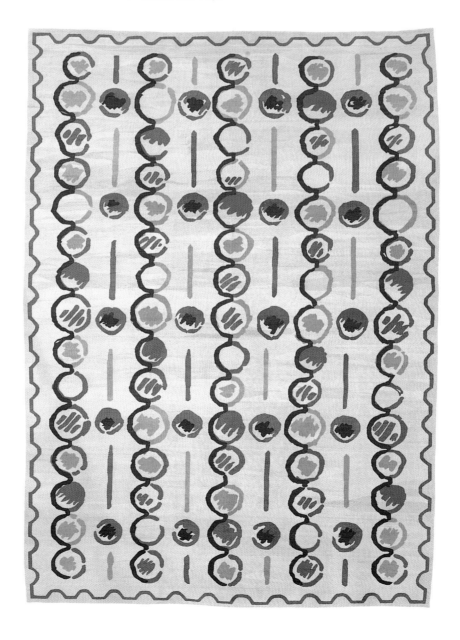

Vincent Dane

Green Park
Handwoven flatweave, wool, 2000
Produced by Robert Stephenson, London, UK
311 × 246 cm (122 × 97 in.)
Courtesy of Robert Stephenson, London, UK

The brief for this rug, and for the example shown on page 83, could have been for a Bessarabian kilim (a traditional Romanian flatweave) combined with a more contemporary feel. It is interesting to note, however, that, although the historical influence is discernible, the artist has gone some distance from his traditional starting point.

Brad Davis (born 1942)
& Janis Provisor (born 1946)

Stripes – Grey
Handknotted wild silk, 1997
Produced by Fort Street Studio, Hong Kong, China
366 × 274 cm (144 × 108 in.)
Private collection, New York, USA

The best rugs, such as this, are so intrinsically beautiful in design and manufacture that they can coexist in the most exquisitely designed rooms containing art and furnishings of the highest quality.

Brad Davis & Janis Provisor

Texture – Green
Handknotted wild silk, 1998
Produced by Fort Street Studio, Hong Kong, China
366 × 274 cm (144 × 108 in.)
Private collection, Milan, Italy

All rugs from Fort Street Studio have been designed by
husband-and-wife team Brad Davis and Janis Provisor.
Each rug is the result of a series of watercolours and a great
deal of editing. These pieces take the art of the carpet to a
new level of artistry that has rarely been achieved in the
past hundred years.

Brad Davis & Janis Provisor

Orbit
Handknotted wild silk, 2000
Produced by Fort Street Studio, Hong Kong, China
366 × 274 cm (144 × 108 in.)
Private collection, London, UK

This design is unusually pictorial for these artists; only a high knot count and a weaver of sublime skill can recreate the sensitivity and fineness of the drawing. The softly blurred edges and colour bleeds are especially pleasing. The title suggests other worlds, and traditionally in the East the carpet has often been symbolic of heavenly spheres.

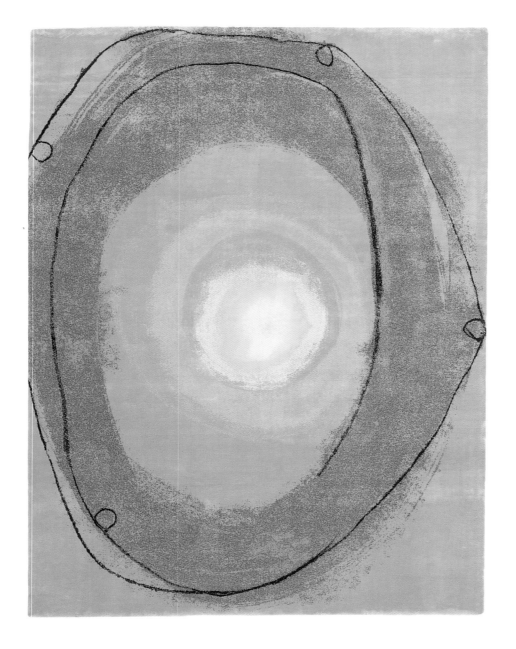

Brad Davis & Janis Provisor

Sidebar – Brown
Handknotted wild silk, 2001
Produced by Fort Street Studio, Hong Kong, China
366 × 274 cm (144 × 108 in.)
Private collection, Hong Kong, China

Why would these highly successful artists leave New York
and take their work to China to be made into silk rugs? After
years of surmounting incredible obstacles, both technical
and human, the results speak for themselves. The artists'
sensibilities and concerns have been elevated and intensely
expressed in carpet form.

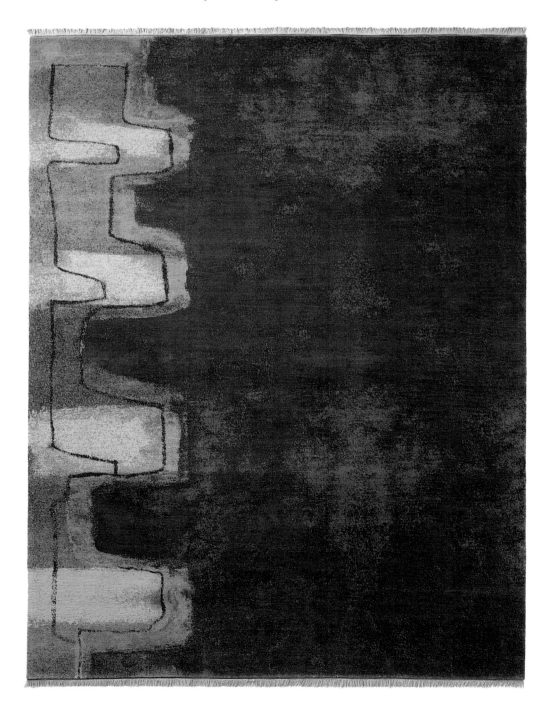

Tom Dixon (born 1959)

Maze
Gun-tufted wool, 1999
Produced by Asplund, Stockholm, Sweden
200 × 200 cm (79 × 79 in.)
Courtesy of Asplund, Stockholm, Sweden

Tom Dixon, one of the most important figures in the world
of product design, renowned for his work with leading
European furniture manufacturers such as the Milanese firm
Cappellini, produced this design for the Swedish company
Asplund. The pattern is, in fact, a continuous line, and
is reminiscent of West African *kuba* cloths (appliquéd textiles
made from natural fibres).

Diane Elson (born 1971)

Albers
Handknotted wool, 1998
Produced by Elson & Co., San Francisco, USA
244 × 300 cm (96 × 108 in.)
Courtesy of Elson & Co., San Francisco, USA

This attractive rug shows what can be achieved with the
use of simple fields of colour even when these are worked
in three shades of red. The asymmetric placement of the
different shades creates a tension, so that a simple design
becomes intriguing.

Diane Elson

Apron
Handknotted wool, 1998
Produced by Elson & Co., San Francisco, USA
244 × 300 cm (96 × 108 in.)
Courtesy of Elson & Co., San Francisco, USA

This rug uses the basic structure of a handknotted rug as the format for the design. All handknotted rugs consist of row upon row of knots that make up the pattern. A weaver would quite easily follow the layout seen here, even though it appears very complicated.

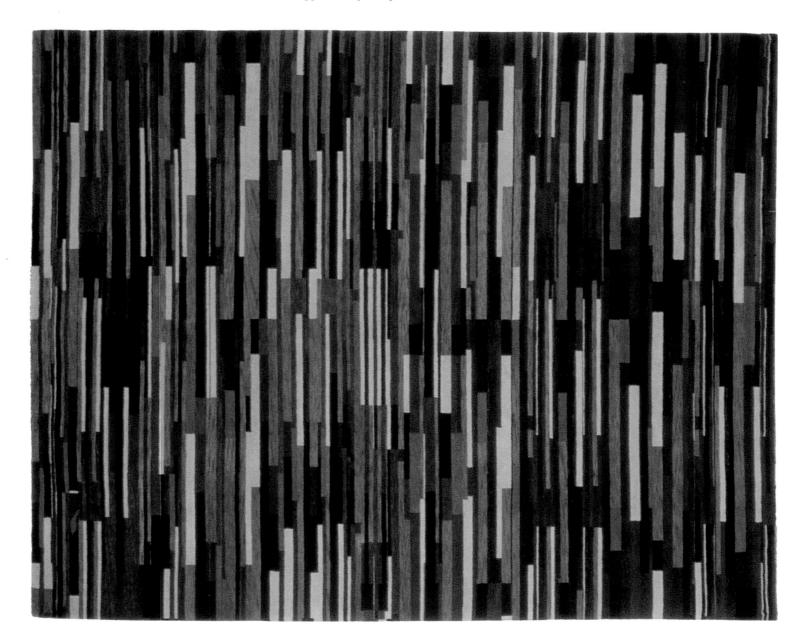

Christopher Farr (born 1953)

Flint
Handknotted wool, 1998
Produced by Christopher Farr, London, UK
244 × 180 cm (96 × 71 in.)
Private collection, London, UK

The aubergine and red of this rug form a colour scheme that
Farr has often used over the years. The design is unusual in
that it is very directional: it appears to be pointing one way
rather than another, much like a prayer rug.

Christopher Farr

Untitled
Handknotted wool, 1992
Produced by Christopher Farr, London, UK
Edition of 10
200 × 200 cm (79 × 79 in.)
Courtesy of John Keatley collection, Cambridgeshire, UK

Here the designer hovers between two distinct styles. The borders and general layout are reminiscent of traditional Southern Iranian tribal weaving, as are the ends and stripey outside borders, yet the explosion of squares is more modern, closer to Constructivism and De Stijl.

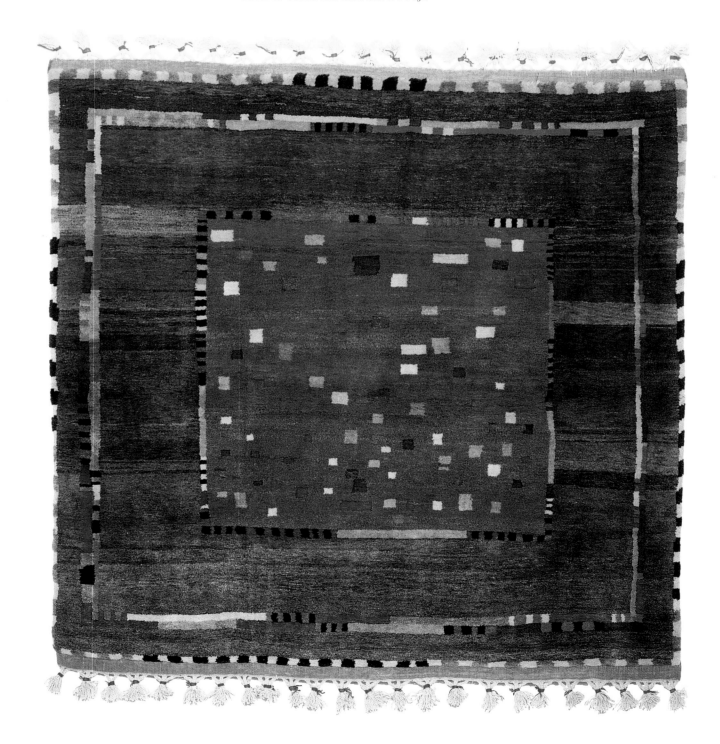

Christopher Farr

181
Handknotted wool, 1994
Produced by Christopher Farr, London, UK
224 × 185 cm (88 × 73 in.)
Private collection, Santiago, Chile

Farr makes no secret of his love of American painting of the past fifty years. In this rug, one of four inspired by the work of the Irish-born but mainly US-based artist Sean Scully, the designer plays down the strength of the design by using only three colours.

Christopher Farr

196
Handknotted wool, 1995
Produced by Christopher Farr, London, UK
200 × 200 cm (79 × 79 in.)
Private collection, Los Angeles, USA

Saturated colour and emotion work together in this rug, where tension is achieved by the placing of two rectangles within a square. These formal concerns echo those of Mark Rothko and Agnes Martin, two of the most prominent post-war painters in the United States. As a rule in minimalist design, whether the focus is architecture, furniture or textiles, the materials have to be of the highest quality.

Christopher Farr

Untitled
Handknotted wool, 1995
Produced by Christopher Farr, London, UK
220 × 150 cm (87 × 59 in.)
Private collection, Los Angeles, USA

This design, from the same collection as the rug shown
opposite, displays the strong influence of twentieth-century
American abstract painting. To add interest, the outlines
have been woven in an intentionally 'haphazard' manner.

Christopher Farr

Untitled
Handknotted wool, 1995
Produced by Christopher Farr, London, UK
210 × 200 cm (83 × 79 in.)
Private collection, New York, USA

Most of Christopher Farr's designs from the 1990s were
produced in very muted colourways, but this fiery red proved
to be one of his most successful designs of the period. For
such simple pieces to be successful the very best materials
must be used. The pile was also hand-trimmed on the loom
to produce a slightly uneven surface.

Christopher Farr

Untitled
Handknotted wool, 1996
Produced by Christopher Farr, London, UK
200 × 200 cm (79 × 79 in.)
Private collection, Munich, Germany

This simple rug allows the high quality of the materials to
make a bold, decorative statement. It is only possible to make
such a simple design work when great attention is paid to
colour combination and proportion. The rug is typical of the
work that both the company and the designer became known
for during the 1990s.

Christopher Farr

Untitled
Handknotted wool, 1996
Produced by Christopher Farr, London, UK
300 × 200 cm (118 × 79 in.)
Private collection, Chicago, USA

Close inspection reveals that this rug is based on a
traditional format: a central field within a relatively
uniform border. The palette of yellow and beige is very
contemporary, and the white lines, which appear to be
laid on top of the border and field arrangement, add
interest. Their freehand appearance is, in fact, fairly
difficult to achieve with the handknotting process.

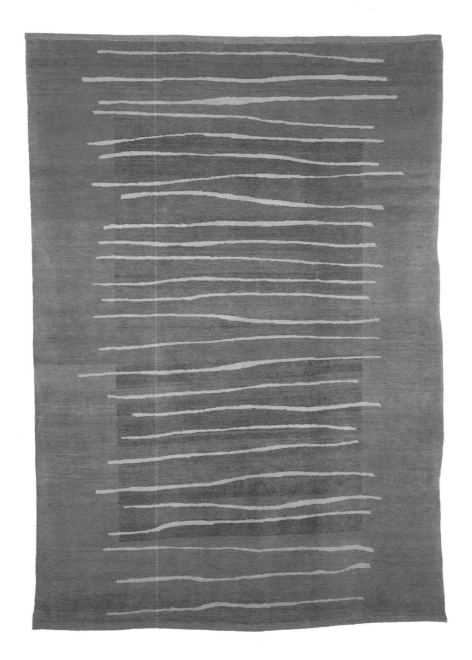

Christopher Farr

Atlas
Handwoven flatweave, wool, 1997
Produced by Christopher Farr, London, UK
Edition of 15
269 × 180 cm (106 × 71 in.)
Private collection, Chicago, USA

'Ethnic' and 'modern' are two themes that collided strongly towards the end of the twentieth century, but this design avoids a clash between the two 'cultures'. The horizontal lines in this flatweave are reminiscent of carved, bone-like forms and have been placed a formal three-colour field background.

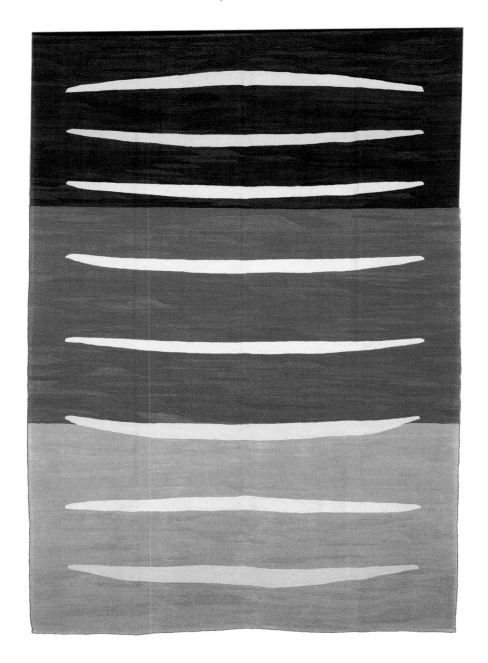

Christopher Farr

Chan Chan
Handknotted wool, 1997
Produced by Christopher Farr, London, UK
274 × 183 cm (108 × 72 in.)
Private collection, London, UK

The main source of this design was a series of drawings made at the Inca fortress in Cuzco, Peru. The tension created by one huge, finely cut stone placed next to another exerts a tremendous force. In this design Farr wanted to achieve a similar effect through the colour and weight of his own material, and endeavoured to get it exactly right.

Christopher Farr

Boardwalk 4
Handknotted wool, 1998
Produced by Christopher Farr, London, UK
213 × 152 cm (84 × 60 in.)
Courtesy of Christopher Farr, London, UK

Today decorative art is as respectable and prestigious as at
any time in the past hundred years, and has shed its early,
sometimes negative connotations. 'Decorative' does not
necessarily mean 'devoid of content', even if the designer's
sole concern is form. This small rug's inspiration is drawn
from studies taken from the natural world.

Christopher Farr

Crimson Tide
Handknotted wool, 1998
Produced by Christopher Farr, London, UK
310 × 215 cm (122 × 85 in.)
Edition of 10
Private collection, Birmingham, Alabama, USA

Introducing a harmony of close tones is a sure way of creating
a feeling of ease, and establishing the mood, when designing
the interior of a room. Here the reds emanate powerfully,
enhanced by the six parabolic forms, which give a sense of
continuous movement.

Christopher Farr

Guggenheim
Handknotted wool, 1998
Produced by Christopher Farr, London, UK
305 × 244 cm (120 × 96 in.)
Private collection, Los Angeles, USA

As the title suggests, this rug has an echo of the celebrated
museum of the same name in New York, designed by Frank
Lloyd Wright. The gentle sweep of the curve creates an
illusion of movement and rounded form when the rug is
placed on the floor, countering the rectangle that contains it.

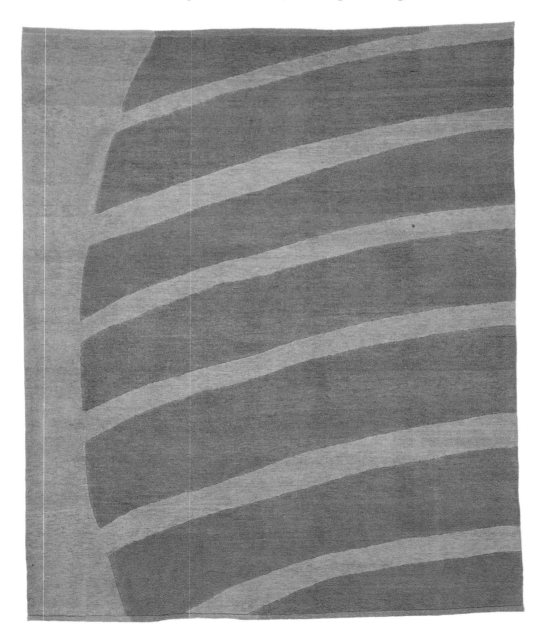

Christopher Farr

Huaras
Handknotted wool, 1998
Produced by Christopher Farr, London, UK
400 × 300 cm (157 × 118 in.)
Courtesy of Christopher Farr, London, UK

Farr is one of the few people in Europe designing large, room-sized rugs that are available 'off the peg'. In recent years rugs such as these have come to be seen as very respectable alternatives to the more traditional Oriental pieces previously seen as the only option by those looking to fill a large amount of floor space. Given that the rug is going to cover such a wide area, Farr keeps it simple in his use of both large areas of colour and a restrained palette.

Christopher Farr

Latitude 6
Handwoven flatweave, wool, 1998
Produced by Christopher Farr, London, UK
310 × 215 cm (122 × 85 in.)
Private collection, Denmark

This flatweave clearly expresses an understanding of the basic
principles of the Bauhaus, which set out to bring together
architecture and the applied arts in a coherent whole, while
allowing each area of design to retain its individuality.

Christopher Farr

Boardwalk 2
Handknotted wool, 1998
Produced by Christopher Farr, London, UK
221 × 150 cm (87 × 59 in.)
Courtesy of Christopher Farr, London, UK

The close, perhaps 'ethnic' tones of this rug are typical of the designer's work towards the end of the twentieth century, and suggest an earthy style of Modernism. This piece can work equally well on its own or with a small, low table placed on its axis or backbone. There are several rugs in Farr's 'Latitude' collection that explore similar themes.

Kaffe Fassett (born 1937)

Untitled
Handknotted wool, 1993
Produced by Christopher Farr, London, UK
Edition of 5
264 × 193 cm (104 × 76 in.)
Collection of Pamela Dressler, Santa Fe, New Mexico, USA

When examined carefully this design appears to be a collage of several rugs stacked up in every direction. Kaffe Fassett has studied Oriental rugs in great depth and understands intimately how patterns and colours coexist. It might seem that there is too much going on, yet this rug proves that it is possible to design a modern rug that has integrity and detail equal to those of an old one.

Kaffe Fassett

Untitled
Handknotted wool, 1994
Produced by Christopher Farr, London, UK
Edition of 15
200 × 280 cm (79 × 110 in.)
Private collection, San Francisco, USA

Kaffe Fassett became renowned for inspiring an enormous
resurgence of interest in knitting throughout the 1980s and
1990s, and in particular championed the use of strong,
saturated colours in striking combinations. This design's
layout has echoes of eighteenth-century Ottoman embroidery.
What is interesting is the way Fassett has designed the shifts
in colour, sometimes inserting just one line of knots to
provide a contrast. This is clearly related to his extensive
knitted work, where his trademark was to introduce
seemingly random colour changes as he went along.

Helmut Federle (born 1944)

Untitled
Handknotted wool, 2001
Produced by Peter Blum, New York, USA
346 × 243 cm (136 × 96 in.)
Courtesy of Peter Blum, New York, USA

Federle is one of Switzerland's most established artists,
known for his abstract paintings of great depth and purity.
This particular image suggests the traces of an ancient
culture, its sophisticated geometry contrasting gracefully
with the rough-hewn tree-like shapes defining the edges.

Stefano Giovannoni (born 1959)

Pluto's Eyes
Gun-tufted wool, 1999
Produced by Asplund, Stockholm, Sweden
250 × 185 cm (98 × 73 in.)
Courtesy of Asplund, Stockholm, Sweden

Disney's cartoon character Pluto inspired the motif for this
rug. While the idea might smack of gimmickry, the ovoid
shapes and their distribution and spacing are innovative.
Nevertheless, the uncompromising nature of the image
could make it difficult to place the rug in an existing
decorative scheme.

Romeo Gigli (born 1949)

String Galaxy
Handwoven flatweave, wool, 1993
Produced by Christopher Farr, London, UK
Edition of 15
300 × 270 cm (118 × 106 in.)
Courtesy of Christopher Farr, London, UK

In the late 1980s and early 1990s Romeo Gigli was considered by many to be one of the finest fashion designers in the world. During this period he was commissioned to design a series of flatweaves that were exhibited at the Salon del Mobile in Milan in 1993. Voted one of the top four things to see that year by *The New York Times*, Gigli's flatweaves took a medium that had become associated with a certain kind of 'ethnic' home-decorating style and reinvented it by the use of extraordinary colour combinations and an extremely imaginative use of the possibilities allowed by the kilim technique. Although this design appears to challenge the traditional pattern language deployed in Eastern flatweaves, its shapes and the large areas of colour in fact play to the strengths of the most important elements of that technique: the use of 'lazy lines' and juxtaposed colour, achieved by the use of finely interlocking wefts.

Adam M.R. Gilchrist (born 1959)

Damascus Shell
Handknotted wool, 1999
Produced by Veedon Fleece, London, UK
100 × 125 cm (39 × 49 in.)
Courtesy of Veedon Fleece, London, UK

Top Shell
Handknotted wool, 2000
Produced by Veedon Fleece, London, UK
100 × 125 cm (39 × 49 in.)
Courtesy of Veedon Fleece, London, UK

Adam Gilchrist has largely confined his company to making reproductions of classical Oriental designs, but recently he has started to work with more contemporary themes. *Damascus Shell*, in particular, shows considerable originality in an area where it is all too easy to adopt a standardized modern look. This design is particularly difficult to execute to a high standard because the waveforms tend to 'fight' with the grid structure that is the warp and weft of a handknotted rug.

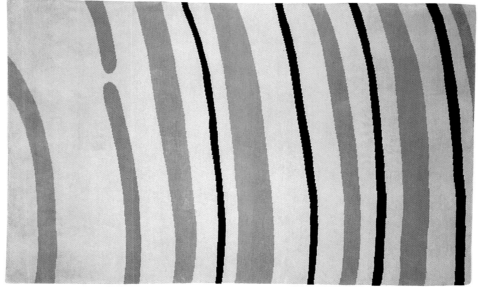

Sally Greaves Lord (born 1957)

Untitled
Handwoven flatweave, wool, 1993
Produced by Christopher Farr, London, UK
Edition of 10
200 × 150 cm (79 × 59 in.)
Private collection, Switzerland

The shadow of the Bauhaus textiles department has encompassed many great designers, including Sally Greaves Lord. This flatweave shows how a designer has absorbed a strong influence and produced a contemporary design that is both sophisticated and highly personal.

Jody Harrow (born 1954)

Rocks at Ise
Gun-tufted wool, 1990
Produced by Tisca, Bordeaux, France
Edition of 10
275 × 180 cm (108 × 71 in.)
Courtesy of Tisca, Bordeaux, France

This rug's highly realistic rendering of a stony beach shows
what can be done with the gun-tufting technique. The varying
height of the pile, the rounded edges of the rocks and the
intricate use of so many soft colours could not have been
achieved by any other method.

Nicky Haslam (born 1939)

Dragonfly
Handknotted wool, 2000
Produced by The Rug Company, London, UK
300 × 220 cm (118 × 87 in.)
Courtesy of The Rug Company, London, UK

Here the renowned interior designer Nicky Haslam shows his experience in planning interior spaces by producing a design that could easily work as a wall-to-wall carpet. The absence of any 'look at me' motif, the soft colour palette and the small, well-spaced pattern allow for easy placement of furniture and artwork.

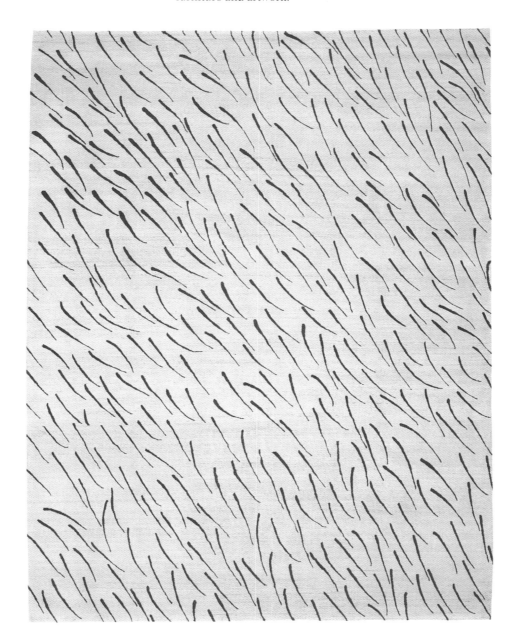

Josef Herman OBE, RA (1911–2000)

Untitled
Handknotted wool, 1994
Produced by Christopher Farr, London, UK
Edition of 10
200 × 152 cm (79 × 60 in.)
Private collection, London, UK

The artist Josef Herman owned one of the world's greatest collections of African miniature sculpture, and many of these pieces surrounded him in his studio. Their influence, however subtly expressed, was undoubtedly profound, for this rug has something of the mystery of African art.

Josef Herman OBE, RA

Untitled
Handknotted wool, 1997
Produced by Christopher Farr, London, UK
Edition of 5
294 × 207 cm (116 × 81 in.)
Collection of Richard and Nicole Joseph, London, UK

One of the late artist's sketchbooks provided the basis for this
design. Over the years Herman made several sketchbooks,
which represented an important aspect of his practice.
Starting each day at dawn or even earlier, he would draw
with ink or crayon, developing themes that included trees
and birds, and often inscribing words at the base of the page.
This rug clearly employs a tree form, which dramatically
occupies the rectangle in an almost architectural manner.

Allegra Hicks (born 1961)

Bindi
Handwoven flatweave, wool, 1995
Produced by Christopher Farr, London, UK
Edition of 15
300 × 200 cm (118 × 79 in.)
Private collection, Paris, France

Part of a collection produced for an exhibition in New York, this design perfectly demonstrates Hicks's innate understanding of the flatweave technique, allowing the natural *abrasch* achieved by painstaking hand-dyeing to do much of the work. Like many of her designs, it is woven 'the wrong way' – in other words, on its length – in order to achieve a fluidity of line. This technique was pioneered by the producers in the mid-1990s.

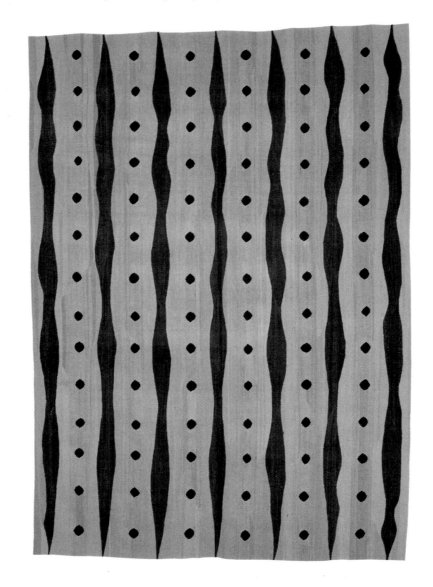

Allegra Hicks

Silver
Handwoven flatweave, wool, 1995
Produced by Christopher Farr, London, UK
370 × 200 cm (146 × 79 in.)
Private collection, London, UK

Produced as a private commission for a London townhouse, this flatweave is unusual in that it lacks borders. This feature, along with the fact that the design is a repeat with the pattern slipping off the edges as if into infinity, gives the impression of a textile or a furnishing fabric rather than a floor covering. The piece illustrates perfectly what Hicks has brought to the field of rug design: an exquisite eye for colour and pattern unimpeded by any preconception of what a rug is supposed to look like.

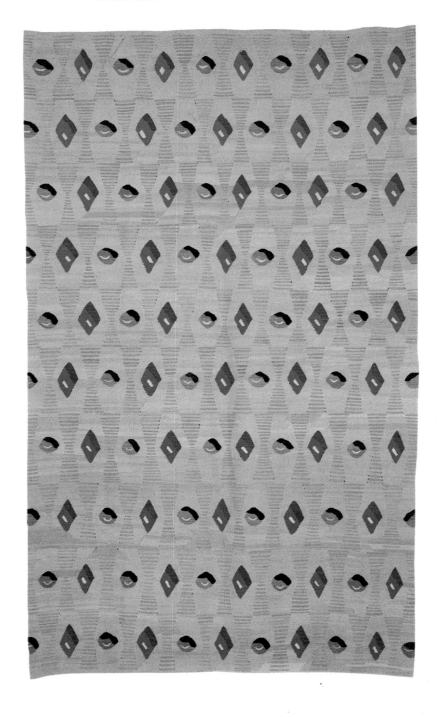

Allegra Hicks

Wave
Handwoven flatweave, wool, 1995
Produced by Christopher Farr, London, UK
Edition of 15
300 × 200 cm (118 × 79 in.)
Private collection, New York, USA

This design is very recognizably the work of Allegra Hicks.
The use of repeat patterns that are informed by traditional
Eastern influences and are at the same time contemporary
has become a trademark of this designer. Her pieces are easily
placed in today's interiors, which often mix the modern and
the antique within the same space. Moreover, the fact that her
designs are often repeats using only three or four colours allows
for easy customizing of the rug into various shapes and sizes.

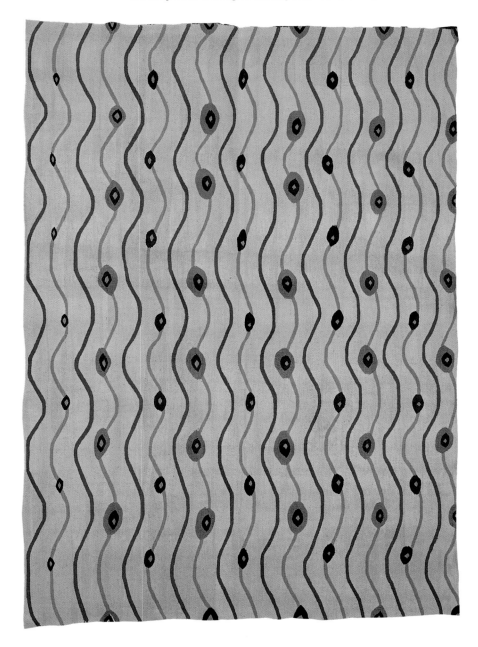

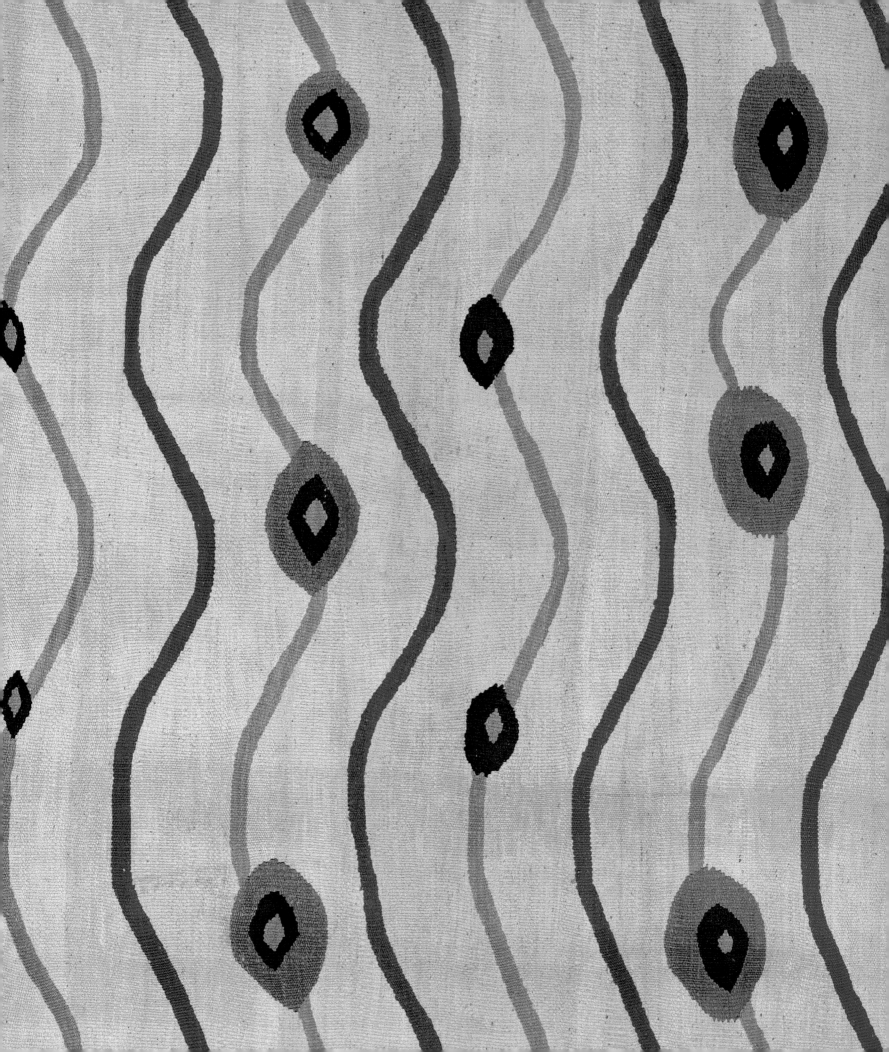

Allegra Hicks

Air
Handknotted wool, 1998
Produced by Christopher Farr, London, UK
Edition of 15
300 × 200 cm (118 × 79 in.)
Private collection, Brussels, Belgium

Allegra Hicks is perhaps best known for her flatweaves, but this is a particularly successful handknotted example of her work. The circular shapes were deliberately drawn freehand, to make sure that each one was different. The background colour was chosen for the beautiful *abrasch* it produces through being hand-dyed and used in a large area.

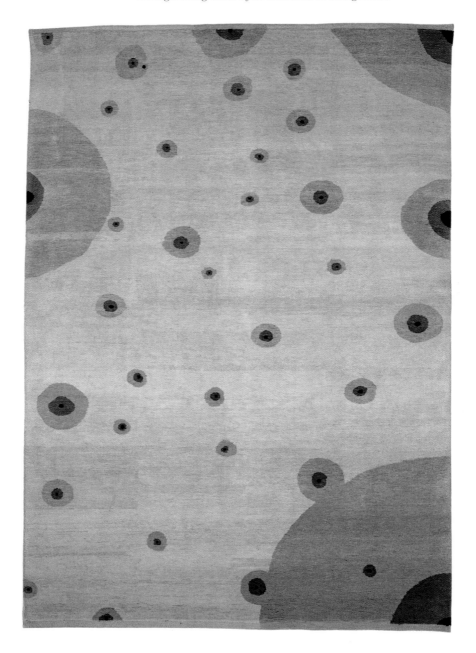

Allegra Hicks

Shadows
Handwoven flatweave, wool, 1998
Produced by Christopher Farr, London, UK
Edition of 15
300 × 200 cm (118 × 79 in.)
Private collection, San Francisco, USA

An overall design has traditionally been the most successful pattern for a rug in a drawing- or dining-room since, whatever the point of access, one part gives you the whole. When furniture is placed on the rug it becomes a playing-field, but even then the piece can have a considerable presence. With a design such as this one it is possible to dictate the mood of the whole interior.

Allegra Hicks

Star
Handknotted wool, 1998
Produced by Christopher Farr, London, UK
Edition of 15
300 × 300 cm (118 × 118 in.)
Private collection, New York, USA

In the rare event of being given the option, the experienced interior designer may well prefer to start with a rug, which then becomes the palette and theme for every decision that follows. This is an inspirational rug that opens up a variety of possibilities for a designer who has a sure touch. The design can work on its own without compromise, although perhaps it would be more interesting to place a chair or a table upon it.

Allegra Hicks

Tree
Handwoven flatweave, wool, 1999
Produced by Christopher Farr, London, UK
Edition of 10
300 × 200 cm (118 × 79 in.)
Courtesy of Christopher Farr, London, UK

Hand-dyeing wool in small quantities produces fine striations of close tones. In this weave three colours have been skilfully employed to maximum effect. The designer thought carefully how the weaver would fill in the space, and, as a consequence, the piece displays a restrained elegance and beauty.

Gary Hume RA (born 1962)

Sky Carpet
Handknotted wool, 1997
Produced by Christopher Farr for White Cube, London, UK
Based on the artist's painting *Sky*, 1997
Edition of 10
300 × 201 cm (118 × 79 in.)
Courtesy of White Cube, London, UK

Looking up through trees in high summer, you may feel inspired as the artist Gary Hume was when he made the painting *Sky*. This rug, when placed on the floor, gently reverses the original view, and in so doing offers a quiet comment on our curious perception of the natural world. The leaves in *Sky Carpet* hark back to traditional carpet design, which drew heavily on flora as a source. Gary Hume's painting *Sky* and rug *Sky Carpet* were shown at the São Paulo Biennale in Brazil in 1997.

Gary Hume RA

Door Rug
Handknotted wool, 2001
Produced by Christopher Farr, London, UK
Design taken from Gary Hume's 'Door paintings' series
Edition of 31
300 × 200 cm (118 × 79 in.)
Courtesy of Christopher Farr, London, UK

A door on the floor. With this rug, metaphor and irony go hand in hand, bringing an enjoyable new dimension to floor covering. An exacting artist, Hume saw that a thoughtful examination of the process of rug-making, as well as the precise hand-carving of the two circles and rectangles of the hospital-door design, was necessary in order to produce perfect proportion and tone. The result is a sublimely beautiful, one-colour rug, which at first glance reveals simple geometry and the play of light, along with shadows cast by the relief elements. And then the fun begins.

James Irvine (born 1958)

Carpet X5
Gun-tufted wool, 1999
Produced by Asplund, Stockholm, Sweden
200 × 160 cm (79 × 63 in.)
Courtesy of Asplund, Stockholm, Sweden

James Irvine, one of a number of British product and
furniture designers who have achieved widespread recognition
over the past ten years or so through collaboration with the
leading modern furniture manufacturers in Milan, here tries
his hand at rug design. Irvine's background is apparent in
the use of rounded forms that are laid out in a balanced and
symmetrical way, while the choice of colours is reminiscent
of the palettes used in recent years in furnishing fabrics.

Bill Jacklin RA (born 1943)

Anemone
Handknotted wool, 1993
Produced by Christopher Farr, London, UK
Edition of 10
200 × 150 cm (79 × 59 in.)
Private collection, London, UK

Jacklin's series of watercolours and etchings of anemones inspired this design, as did his abiding interest in Islamic art. The latter is evident in the freely drawn 'running dog' border, which sets off the floating anemone motifs to great effect. The rich, jewel-like colour is also reminiscent of a great tribal rug from the Near East.

Bill Jacklin RA

Anemone 1
Handknotted wool, 1993
Produced by Christopher Farr, London, UK
Edition of 10
200 × 150 cm (79 × 59 in.)
Collection of the artist, New York, USA

This is the first in a series of six rugs based on the theme of falling petals. The floral shapes are transformed into soaring, almost brutal jagged forms. Any sentimental prettiness is cleverly sidestepped by a border that looks like a castle battlement, with which the petals cannot fail to create an arresting visual tension.

Sandy Jones (born 1946)

Zennor
Handknotted wool, 1993
Produced by Christopher Farr, London, UK
Edition of 10
400 × 330 cm (157 × 130 in.)
Private collection, London, UK

Sandy Jones designed a collection of large rugs for the
London-based company Christopher Farr, which were
exhibited at the Royal College of Art in 1993. At that time this
was the only collection of its type on the European market,
as contemporary producers were generally reluctant to make
such large pieces 'on spec'. Jones had years of experience
in designing furnishings for some of the finest houses in the
world, and was very keen to develop a contemporary look
that would stand comparison with the great Oriental carpets
that had traditionally been used in such projects.

Sandy Jones

Prussia
Handknotted wool, 1994
Produced by Christopher Farr, London, UK
Edition of 10
400 × 340 cm (157 × 134 in.)
Private collection, London, UK

This design has the same feel as *Zennor*, opposite, but here
Jones has deployed the use of borders to contain the pattern.
After thinking carefully about how furniture could be placed
on these large rugs, the designer decided to use a slightly
zoned layout.

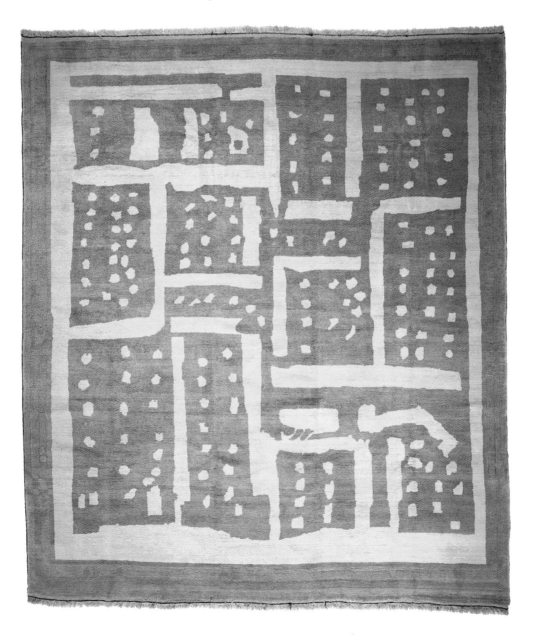

Sandy Jones

Untitled
Handknotted with handwoven flatweave side borders,
   wool, 1994
Produced by Christopher Farr, London, UK
425 × 252 cm (167 × 99 in.)
Private collection, Athens, Greece

This rug plays a pivotal role in a London apartment of
grand proportions. It has a pile field and a flatweave border,
which emphasize its sculptural, almost architectural quality.
The apparently simple design becomes less so as one looks
closely at the carefully controlled colour and the unexpected
placing of the blue stripes.

Sandy Jones

Untitled
Handknotted with handwoven flatweave, wool, 1996
Produced by Christopher Farr, London, UK
Both 300 × 90 cm (118 × 35 in.)
Private collection, Athens, Greece

Sandy Jones created these designs as a commission for a large
private residence. They employ a technique developed with the
producers over the past ten years, whereby handknotting and
flatweave are combined in one piece to give a relief to the design.
In these examples, knotted pile is used for the horizontal yellow
stripes in the rug on the left, and for the blue vertical stripes in
the rug on the right. All other areas are in flatweave.

Jan Kath (born 1972)

Cubus
Handknotted wool, 2000
Produced by Jan Kath Carpets, Bochum, Germany
260 × 180 cm (102 × 71 in.)
Courtesy of Jan Kath Carpets, Bochum, Germany

The use in this rug of a well-known optical device has the
advantage of producing an interesting all-over pattern that
is nevertheless easy to incorporate in existing decorative
schemes. A high degree of precision was required in the
weaving, as the whole pattern relies on an accurate repeat.
Close inspection reveals small variations in each of the
'blocks'; this is certainly unintentional but adds interest.

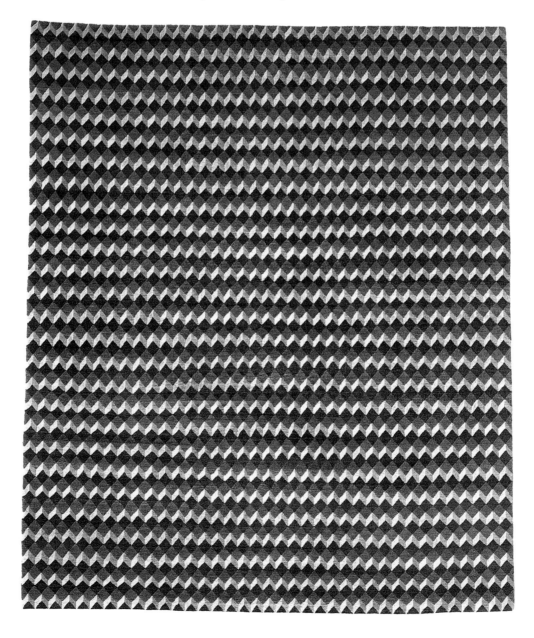

Jan Kath

Oppart
Handknotted wool, 1997
Produced by Jan Kath Carpets, Bochum, Germany
250 × 200 cm (98 × 79 in.)
Courtesy of Jan Kath Carpets, Bochum, Germany

In contemplating this rug, the viewer initially has the
impression of looking at the work of a machine or a screen
print. It is hard to imagine from a photograph that it is a rug
made up of thousands of individual knots. The design, inspired
by the Op Art movement of the 1960s, is softened by the use
of gentle colours. It is also reversed out, providing even
greater visual interest.

Jan Kath

Vario II
Handknotted wool, 2000
Produced by Jan Kath Carpets, Bochum, Germany
240 × 170 cm (95 × 67 in.)
Courtesy of Jan Kath Carpets, Bochum, Germany

This whole rug teases the eye and intrigues the mind as it
follows the effortless logic of the design. It is hard to imagine
a more pleasing medium in which to explore a labyrinth.
The whiteness made up of two distinct shades is the key to its
success, as one's perception of the drawing fades in and out.

Jan Kath

Vario II
Handknotted wool, 2000
Produced by Jan Kath Carpets, Bochum, Germany
200 × 200 cm (79 × 79 in.)
Courtesy of Jan Kath Carpets, Bochum, Germany

Using different pile heights to produce a subtle design is a
device that was increasingly common towards the end of the
1990s. This example is particularly successful and would
perhaps have been too jarring to the eye if the more
traditional method of juxtaposing colours had been used.

Behrouz Kolahi (born 1954)

Microchip 5B
Handknotted wool, 1998
Produced by Battilossi & Kolahi, Editori Italiani di Tappeti, Turin, Italy
270 × 160 cm (106 × 63 in.)
Courtesy of Battilossi & Kolahi, Editori Italiani di Tappeti, Turin, Italy

A fascinating fusion of high technology and ancient craft, the design of this striking handknotted rug was taken from the layout of a microchip enlarged thousands of times. Interestingly, the layout and proportions echo the 'Pomegranate' design found in eighteenth- and nineteenth-century Kotan carpets from east Turkestan.

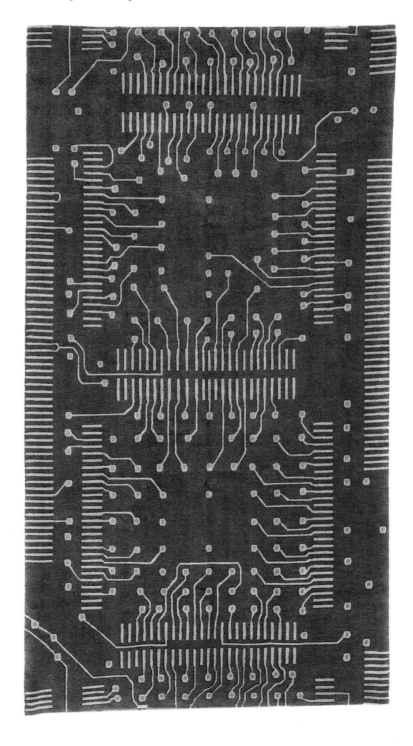

Jonas Lindvall (born 1963)

Pattern in Relief
Gun-tufted wool, 1996
Produced by Asplund, Stockholm, Sweden
210 × 160 cm (83 × 63 in.)
Courtesy of Asplund, Stockholm, Sweden

Maze-like patterns such as these were first seen in the 1920s and 1930s, particularly in the work of Eileen Gray and Evelyn Wyld. Here the comparatively recent technology of gun-tufting allows the design to be successfully rendered in one colour, with certain areas of the pile being clipped lower than others to reveal a counterbalanced structure of shapes at ninety-degree angles. The design would not be so pleasing had two colours and one pile height been used.

Marni

Cube
Handknotted wool, 2000
Produced by The Rug Company, London, UK
230 × 150 cm (91 × 59 in.)
Courtesy of The Rug Company, London, UK

The strong colours and bold design of this rug would make it the main focus of any room and would not allow for easy placement of furniture. Marni, a leading European fashion company, adapted this design from an existing pattern that had previously been used for its garments.

Precious McBane
Meriel Scott (born 1969)
& Evlynn Smith (born 1962)

Blush
Handknotted wool, 2000
Produced by Christopher Farr, London, UK
Edition of 10
250 × 180 cm (98 × 71 in.)
Courtesy of Gary Hume and Georgie Hopton, London, UK

Meriel Scott and Evlynn Smith have not lost sight of a rug's
most pleasing aspect: its appeal to all the senses, particularly
touch. At the forefront of these designers' thinking is the
movement of the body on the rug and how the pink is revealed
as the pile is disturbed. Cutting the pile at different lengths and
using high-lustre wool and mohair together achieve this. There
is an echo here (albeit probably unconscious) of the 'bed rugs'
of the Near East, and this relates strongly to the way we live
now, closer to the floor.

Ulf Moritz (born 1939)

Santana
Needlepoint, wool, 1998
Produced by Kappa Lambda, London, UK
200 × 200 cm (79 × 79 in.)
Courtesy of Kappa Lambda, London, UK

Moritz's needlepoint rug in very subtle tones almost has the
look of a natural floor covering such as seagrass or bouclé.
Although the palette is very neutral, the use of different grid
layouts within each square stops it becoming bland.

Sarah Morris (born 1967)

Midtown – Condé Nast
Handknotted wool, 2001
Produced by Christopher Farr, London, UK
Based on Sarah Morris's original painting
  Midtown – Condé Nast, 1998
Edition of 25
245 × 245 cm (96 × 96 in.)
Courtesy of Christopher Farr, London, UK

The design for this rug was taken from a painting of the side of a skyscraper in Manhattan, yet the work is probably destined for use on the floor. This concept takes the rug beyond formalism, lending the piece an edgy and unexpected quality. Important here are the angle of the grid and the choice of colours. The friction between the precise, hard image and the slow, seductive process of the weaving gives the rug an unforgettable presence.

Nelly Munthe (born 1947)

Waves
Handwoven flatweave, wool, 1993
Produced by the Asad Co. Ltd, London, UK
Edition of 10
200 × 150 cm (79 × 59 in.)
Private collection, Paris, France

This flatweave is both lyrical and suggestive, true to its given title. The artist has an exemplary grasp of the technical strengths and limitations of the weavers, whom she knows well. The result is convincing, owing to the design's simplicity and restraint.

Ralph Nelson (born 1960)
& Raveevarn Choksombatchai (born 1959)

Folded Plate
Gun-tufted wool, 1998
Produced by Elson & Co., San Francisco, USA
183 × 122 cm (72 × 48 in.)
Courtesy of Elson & Co., San Francisco, USA

Ralph Nelson and Raveevarn Choksombatchai were
commissioned by Elson as part of a collaboration with various
architects on the west coast of America. It is interesting that
the architects' approach should be to try to change the rug's
original symmetrical shape, be it circle, square or rectangle,
into an asymmetrical format.

Olly & Suzi (both born 1968)

Rush Hour
Handknotted wool, 2001
Produced by Christopher Farr, London, UK
Edition of 9
272 × 203 cm (107 × 80 in.)
Courtesy of Christopher Farr, London, UK

The inspiration for this rug came from a painting made in the Galapagos Islands by these two nomadic artists. The ancient rhythm of the turtles moving across the sands has an echo in the rhythmic beating of the loom by the weavers, forever tying and cutting their knots. As the artists have plotted the turtles' movements, so have the Turkish cartoon-makers who received the drawing and painstakingly made it ready for the weavers.

Rifat Ozbek (born 1953)

Stripe
Handwoven flatweave, wool, 1995
Produced by Christopher Farr, London, UK
Edition of 15
300 × 200 cm (118 × 79 in.)
Collection of Cindy White, London, UK

Stripe formed part of a collection designed by Ozbek for Christopher Farr in 1995 that was exhibited as a dramatic installation in a derelict garage in London's Chelsea. Ozbek, a world-renowned fashion designer of Turkish origin, combines a highly developed colour sense with an instinctive understanding of the ancient craft of handweaving that is part of his cultural heritage. Christopher Farr's production is itself based in Turkey.

Rifat Ozbek

Untitled
Handknotted wool, 1995
Produced by Christopher Farr, London, UK
Edition of 15
300 × 200 cm (118 × 79 in.)
Collection of Cindy White, London, UK

Ozbek here creates his own version of the *Cintamani* design, a motif in the shape of lips, first seen in twelfth-century Chinese porcelain, which subsequently became popular with Chinese carpet-makers and then spread west to Turkey, where it was a popular design from the fifteenth century. Ozbek has updated the design by removing formal border arrangements and using a fresh, contemporary palette.

Verner Panton (1926–1998)

Square Rug
Handknotted wool, 2000
Produced by Christopher Farr, London, UK. Courtesy of
    Marianne Panton
Edition of 10
One of five patterns from Verner Panton's first collection,
    'Décor', for mira-x in 1969
246 × 246 cm (97 × 97 in.)
Collection of Richard and Nicole Joseph, London, UK

This wonderful rug works in the most acutely designed
surroundings. More surprising, however, is the design's
historical link to the *Gabbeh* rugs of southern Iran. Despite
his legendary innovativeness and modernity, the designer
must have enjoyed his commonality with the nomadic
tribal artists of that region.

Ian Jesson Phin

Untitled
Handknotted with handwoven flatweave end borders, wool, 1991
Produced by Christopher Farr, London, UK
Edition of 10
269 × 178 cm (106 × 70 in.)
Collection of Jerry Reynolds, Somerset, UK

Designed by Ian Phinn when he was a student at the Royal
College of Art in London, this was one of the best rugs to
come out of the exhibition *Brave New Rugs*, held at the college
in 1991. There is no doubt that the work of the artist Paul Klee
was uppermost in the designer's mind at the time. Given such
a strong influence, any student is likely to create a superficial
pastiche, yet it is clear that the designer has found his own way
with this piece.

Michael Rainsford (born 1955)

Untitled
Handknotted wool, 1994
Produced by Christopher Farr, London, UK
Edition of 10
200 × 150 cm (79 × 59 in.)
Private collection, Berlin, Germany

Here the artist has, perhaps unconsciously, designed an Islamic prayer rug, disguised with loose, tonal colours that almost have the effect of camouflage. The design originated in a long series of paintings on paper made with mud from the North Yorkshire Moors. The rug-making process has a quality of earthiness that struck an immediate chord with the artist.

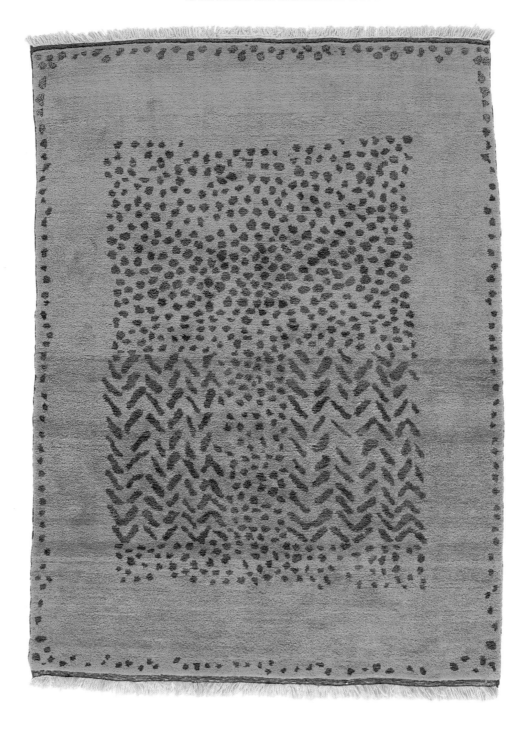

Rex Ray (born 1958)

Fourth Caller
Handknotted wool, 1998
Produced by Elson & Co., San Francisco, USA
300 × 244 cm (108 × 96 in.)
Courtesy of Elson & Co., San Francisco, USA

A very seductive colour combination and a well-balanced
and proportioned design come together in this rug. One
could easily place furniture on it, although it is strong
enough to occupy a space on its own. Rugs that employ
amorphous fields of colour such as this example are,
generally, only successful when woven on a large room-size
format that allows the movement within each colour to
become apparent.

David Shaw Nicholls (born 1959)

Hiran
Handwoven flatweave, wool, 1996
Produced by Nicholls, New York, USA
366 × 274 cm (144 × 108 in.)
Private collection, New York, USA

The architect who designed this flatweave was a student of
Ettore Sottsass, the founder of the Memphis design studio in
the 1980s, and the piece clearly draws on this source. The rug
has an almost heraldic, graphic power, appealing to a knowing
and design-literate audience.

David Shaw Nicholls

Badoura
Handwoven flatweave and looped pile, wool, 1999
Produced by Nicholls, New York, USA
366 × 274 cm (144 × 108 in.)
Private collection, New York, USA

In this rug a balance is achieved between the geometric
design and the soft handling of the chosen medium. The
designer may well have had the intention of designing for
a corporate interior with limited space, where the rug has
to behave itself and play a secondary role. The use of
monochrome colour is kept interesting through the varied
tones created by the slow hand-dyeing process. Two different
pile heights bring light and shadow into play to great effect.

Michael Sodeau (born 1969)

Macassar
Handwoven flatweave, wool, 1998
Produced by Christopher Farr, London, UK
Edition of 15
240 × 180 cm (94 × 71 in.)
Private collection, London, UK

This was Michael Sodeau's first design for Christopher Farr, and
is intended to explore the concept of floor rugs that mimic the
surface appearance of other materials, such as stone or wood. It
has the dark, close-grained texture of tropical wood.

Michael Sodeau

Walking on Water
Handknotted wool, 1998
Produced by Christopher Farr, London, UK
Edition of 15
250 × 190 cm (98 × 75 in.)
Courtesy of Christopher Farr, London, UK

At the end of the 1990s Michael Sodeau produced three
designs for Christopher Farr that explored the nature of
surfaces – specifically, water, stone and wood – in an attempt
to reproduce their essence in an object that would then be laid
on another surface, the floor. This design is taken from a
tracing of the ripples on the surface of a pool of water.

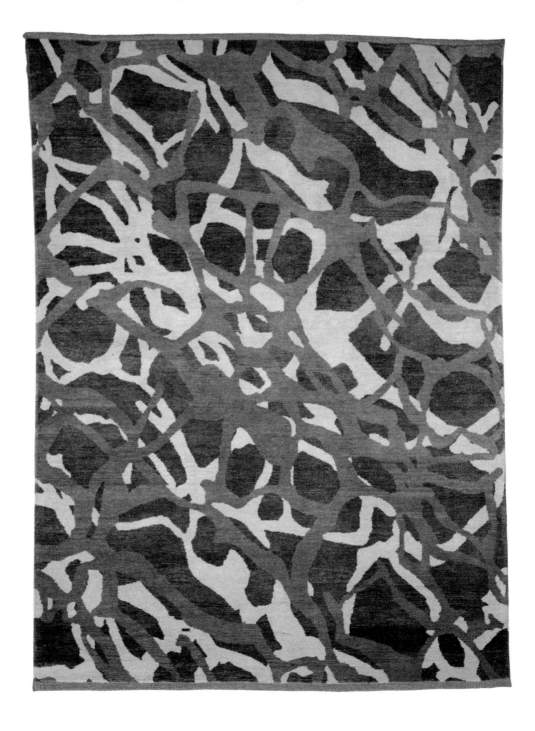

Michael Sodeau

Blue Rug
Looped pile, wool, 2000
Produced by Christopher Farr, London, UK
Edition of 10
300 × 100 cm (118 × 39 in.)
Courtesy of Christopher Farr, London, UK

Continuing the theme of different surfaces (see pp. 164–65), this rug represents 'stone'. The looped effect was achieved by wrapping high-quality wool around a continuous piece of cord many metres long that was then worked into and out of a wool foundation. The technique, which is carried out entirely by hand, was developed specifically for this design.

Agneta Svensk (born 1952)

Ariadne
Handknotted wool, 2001
Produced by the Asad Co. Ltd, London, UK
Edition of 10
203 × 199 cm (80 × 78 in.)
Courtesy of the artist

Here Svensk has embraced the living weaving skills and
traditions of Turkey partly to compensate for the demise of
Sweden's own weaving past. Her design is loosely drawn from
the Greek myth of Ariadne, and the suggestion of a labyrinth
that can be explored freely gives an edge to what might
appear at first glance to be merely decorative.

Agneta Svensk

Fatima
Handwoven flatweave, wool, 2001
Produced by the Asad Co. Ltd, London, UK
Edition of 10
133 × 216 cm (52 × 85 in.)
Courtesy of the artist

In a design that plays to the strengths of the flatweave technique,
the blues and off-whites are streaked with the irregularities of the
slow hand-dyeing process. This Swedish textile designer takes
evident joy in working with Islamic culture, frequently drawing
upon the themes of Turkish weavers.

Agneta Svensk

Pomegranate
Handknotted wool, 2001
Produced by the Asad Co. Ltd, London, UK
Edition of 10
93 × 76 cm (37 × 30 in.)
Courtesy of the artist

A fruit of mythic status in the East, the pomegranate is here abstracted to create a striking design motif for a rug. The piece is a celebration of rich, exotic colour, with pomegranate forms playing off the deep background.

Rosemarie Trockel (born 1952)

Plus – Minus
Handknotted wool, 1987
Produced by Equator Productions, New York, USA
Edition 6
Size 266 × 140 cm (105 × 55 in.)
Courtesy of the artist

Rosemarie Trockel, one of the leading artists in Germany, explores many different media. Textiles have played an important part in her work, which has questioned the status of this medium within the art world. Until recently rug design held a relatively lowly position compared with other fields of creativity, but the attention of such highly regarded artists is gradually changing public perception.

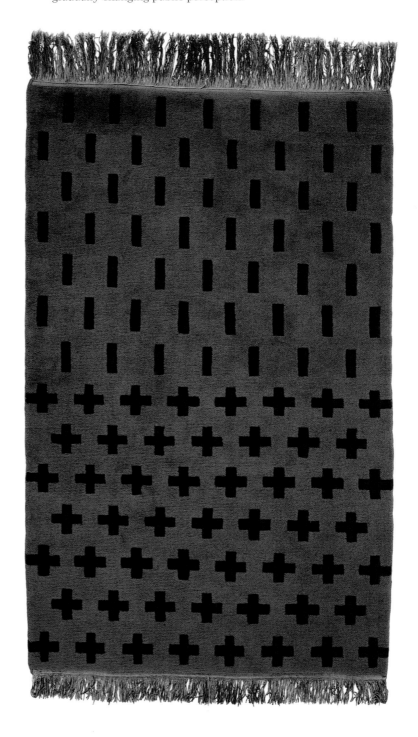

Rosemarie Trockel

Untitled
Handwoven flatweave, wool, 1998
Produced by James Brown, Oaxaca, Mexico
Edition of 6
455 × 163 cm (179 × 64 in.)
Courtesy of the artist

As with Trockel's *Plus – Minus* rug (opposite), this flatweave has an elegant simplicity that contains a subtle suggestion of dualism. The contrasted concepts expressed in these woven images might relate to gender, our experience of time, or simply positive versus negative. While our interest is provoked as to their meaning, we are seduced by their beauty.

Sian Tucker (born 1958)

Untitled
Handknotted wool, 1991
Produced by Christopher Farr, London, UK
Edition of 10
224 × 150 cm (88 × 59 in.)
Courtesy of Christopher Farr, London, UK

This rug displays various elements typical of Sian Tucker's work at the time it was designed, including strong colour combinations and the varied use of a single motif (in this case, a triangle). These motifs form compartments that can be viewed as designs within designs. Tucker produced many painted banners and other textiles using a similar vocabulary.

Sian Tucker

Untitled
Handknotted wool, 1992
Produced by Christopher Farr, London, UK
Edition of 10
240 × 150 cm (94 × 59 in.)
Private collection, London, UK

There is a playful, almost childlike quality to this design, and also perhaps an unconscious reference to the nomadic tribal weavers of the Near East. It is likely, however, that Tucker has simply taken a slightly softer, more relaxed approach to the hard-edge geometry with which she is usually associated. To a designer, the softening of hard edges is a key attraction of the rug-making process.

Gavin Turk (born 1967)

Cave Rug
Handknotted wool, 2001
Produced by Christopher Farr, London, UK
Edition of 5
245 cm (96 in.) diam.
Collection of The British Council, London, UK

Gavin Turk came to prominence during the mid-1990s as part of a group of British artists who went on to stage the controversial and important *Sensation* exhibition at the Royal Academy, London, in 1999. This rug is taken from the plaque he made based on those seen on the façades of London houses of distinguished former residents. His examiners on the MA course at the Royal College of Art famously failed him when he submitted the piece for his degree show. The plaque has since gone on to become iconic, and, when Turk was asked to consider extending his repertoire to rugs, this was the image he chose. Owing to the need for a finer weave for the writing, a cotton rather than a wool foundation was used. In the plaque the white of the letters was slightly indented, and this was reproduced on the rug, by hand-clipping those areas once the piece had come off the loom. Generally, round rugs such as these are first made as squares and then fashioned into circles as part of the finishing process, as was the case with this piece.

AVIN TUR

Sculptor

worked here

1989 – 1991

Georgina von Etzdorf (born 1955)

Giraffe
Handwoven flatweave, wool, 1997
Produced by Christopher Farr, London, UK
Edition of 15
275 × 85 cm (108 × 33 in.)
Private collection, New York, USA

The fluid ribbon design on this runner could only have been achieved so successfully by using the flatweave technique, which lends itself very well to sharp, defined lines. It is clearly the work of Georgina von Etzdorf, one of the most influential textile designers of recent times.

Georgina von Etzdorf

Colour Woven Border
Handwoven flatweave, wool, 1997
Produced by Christopher Farr, London, UK
Edition of 15
274 × 85 cm (108 × 33 in.)
Private collection, Munich, Germany

Once you remove the tooth-like forms from this striking flatweave you are left with an elegant design, not dissimilar from the Chinese yin–yang symbol. With these two elements integrated there is a pleasing optical sensation as the eye and brain process the relatively complex information.

Georgina von Etzdorf

Nirvana Green
Handwoven flatweave, wool, 1997
Produced by Christopher Farr, London, UK
Edition of 15
200 × 200 cm (79 × 79 in.)
Private collection, New York, USA

Compared with the example shown on page 177, this rug shows a more geometric approach. The long, vertical stripes have tested the skill of the weaver, as the technique is best suited to long, horizontal runs of weft. However, the movement of colour in the green areas, which was produced by careful use of 'lazy lines', is very pleasing.

Georgina von Etzdorf

Nirvana Red
Handwoven flatweave, wool, 1997
Produced by Christopher Farr, London, UK
Edition of 15
200 × 200 cm (79 × 79 in.)
Private collection, London, UK

This flatweave design based on the square is not as simple as
it looks. Each colour has been precisely chosen to recede from
or expand into the predominantly red-toned background. The
yellow square dispels any risk of blandness and provides a
welcome discordant note. While the style is reminiscent of
Bauhaus and 1960s design, it is not confined to either period.

Pia Wallen (born 1957)

Carpet Dot
Gun-tufted wool, 2001
Produced by Asplund, Stockholm, Sweden
260 × 150 cm (102 × 59 in.)
Courtesy of Asplund, Stockholm, Sweden

The spacing and size of the dots on this rug and the one
shown opposite are essentially the same, yet the latter seems
more sophisticated. The use there of clipped pile to create
counterbalanced levels is more successful than the use here
of two colours and one pile height. This is ironic, given that
many would consider bright orange to be far from sophisticated.

Pia Wallen

Carpet Convex/Concave
Gun-tufted wool, 1997
Produced by Asplund, Stockholm, Sweden
180 × 80 cm (71 × 31 in.)
Courtesy of Asplund, Stockholm, Sweden

Madeline Weinrib (born 1960)

Kali
Handknotted wool, 1998
Produced by ABC Carpet & Home, New York, USA
Edition of 25
366 × 274 cm (144 × 108 in.)
Courtesy of ABC Carpet & Home, New York, USA

The sensitive use of line-drawing in dividing and compartmentalizing space is shown to great effect in this elegant rug. Painter Madeline Weinrib has clearly studied Japanese textiles and has an acute understanding of how the reading of line is affected by the movement of the surface of the rug.

Madeline Weinrib

Bodi Tree
Handknotted wool, 1998
Produced by ABC Carpet & Home, New York, USA
Edition of 25
366 × 274 cm (144 × 108 in.)
Courtesy of ABC Carpet & Home, New York, USA

The artist reveals her deep love for and understanding of the
Islamic world in this contemporary take on the Tree of Life
prayer rug. The freely drawn forms have an unmistakably
modern sensibility that now has great appeal.

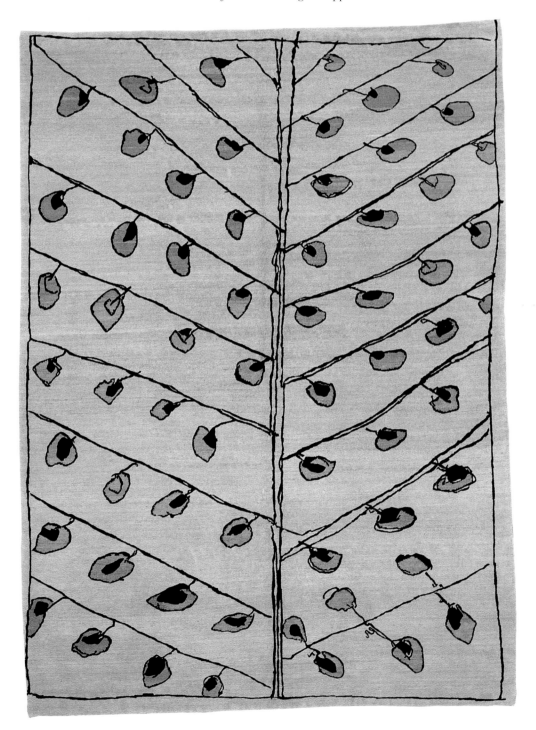

Yukinori Yanagi (born 1959)

The Chrysanthemum Carpet
Handknotted wool and inset metal, 1995
Produced by Peter Blum, New York, USA
1188 × 640 cm (468 × 252 in.)
Courtesy of The National Gallery of Australia, Canberra, Australia

This brilliant-red wool chrysanthemum carpet acted as the central piece of an installation designed for the Peter Blum Gallery, New York, in 1995. Resembling the design of a Japanese passport, which is imprinted with the imperial chrysanthemum crest, *The Chrysanthemum Carpet* metaphorically transports viewers to an arena where conflicts of identity and nationality in post-war Japan are dramatically played out. Yanagi reveals the illusion of the Japanese nation-family united under the emperor, who is represented by the iconic chrysanthemum flower, and exposes the sharp duality of nationality and individual identity within contemporary Japanese society. Woven into the underside of the carpet is the text of Articles 19, 20 and 21 of the Japanese constitution: codes that govern rarely enacted freedoms of thought, religion, speech and assembly.

Helen Yardley (born 1954)

Arc Nero
Gun-tufted wool, 1997
Produced by Helen Yardley, London, UK
270 × 180 cm (106 × 71 in.)
Courtesy of A–Z Studios, London, UK

Helen Yardley's visit, early in her career, to the textile study collection at London's Victoria and Albert Museum has had a telling influence. The shadow cast by Marion Dorn has been a fruitful one, as is shown by this rug – a beautiful piece that both effortlessly absorbs the past and has a strong appeal to today's sophisticated consumer.

Helen Yardley

Rimini Gold
Gun-tufted wool, 1997
Produced by Helen Yardley, London, UK
270 × 180 cm (106 × 71 in.)
Courtesy of A–Z Studios, London, UK

There are few designers with as much experience and ability
as Helen Yardley who have designed almost exclusively for
the floor. In this piece the forms and colours seem effortlessly
placed, while the circles and rectangles occupying a larger
rectangle elegantly counterpoint one another, evoking
tensions and a mood that justifies the somewhat flowery title.

Michael Young

Green Rug
Handknotted wool, 2000
Produced by Christopher Farr, London, UK
Edition of 15
250 × 180 cm (98 × 71 in.)
Courtesy of Christopher Farr, London, UK

Michael Young has been one of the most influential furniture designers since the early 1990s. The palette deployed in this rug is typical of Young's bold, modern approach. The effect of horizontal bands of colour bisected by vertical channels is achieved by clipping two rows of knots lower than the rest.

Marcel Zelmanovitch (born 1951)

Hackney Empire
Handknotted wool, 1993
Produced by Galerie Diurne, Paris, France
240 × 170 cm (94 × 67 in.)
Courtesy of Galerie Diurne, Paris, France

Zelmanovitch has his own rug-making studio in Kathmandu, Nepal,
and his complete understanding of each of the many processes shines
through in his designs. Architecture is a traditional theme
in designs for the floor, dating back to pre-Roman times. Here the
architectural theme is deployed so that the design works in all
directions. Particularly notable is the sensitive and restrained use
of the two reds and two whites.

Marcel Zelmanovitch

Sol 04 01
Handknotted wool, 1999
Produced by Galerie Diurne, Paris, France
270 × 220 cm (106 × 87 in.)
Courtesy of Galerie Diurne, Paris, France

This rug speaks eloquently of the crucial importance of having exactly the right tone, proportion and weave. Its main virtue is its absolute rightness in each of these respects.

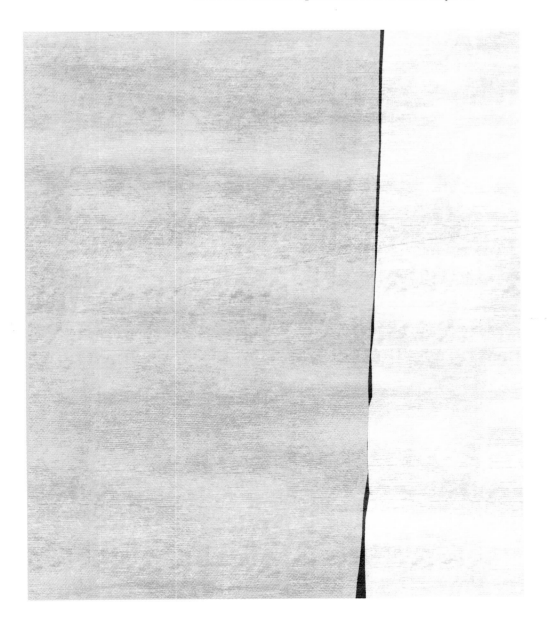

A–Z Studios London, UK
Helen Yardley
Born UK, 1954

Helen Yardley studied textiles in Manchester and at the Royal College of Art, London. Her work is held in collections at the Victoria and Albert Museum and the Crafts Council, both in London. Her design studio has been established for more than seventeen years and has produced carpets for major corporate clients. Yardley has also designed collections for the retail market. Her work has been inspired by an illustrious quartet of British and American designers from the twentieth century, including Evelyn Wyld, Eileen Gray, Marion Dorn and Marian Pepler. Yardley has absorbed the legacy and taken it further, creating work that is both beautiful and beyond mere surface decoration. A carpet in the foyer of a chic hotel or modern office building can play a major part in creating the right ambience. Few architects or designers really understand this; Yardley is one who does.

Angela Adams
Born USA, 1965

Adams's started her design career as a decorative painter. As her horizons broadened she searched for new media in which to express herself, and the strong tradition in Maine of handmade textiles and floor coverings led her to experiment with gun-tufting rugs. This in turn resulted in Adams establishing her own production facility in 1998. She has brought her own distinctive approach to bear on a market where it is sometimes hard to tell one product from another, and ownership of production has allowed her to experiment boldly with techniques while maintaining rigorous control of quality.

Asplund Stockholm, Sweden
Michael Asplund
Born Sweden, 1957
Thomas Asplund
Born Sweden, 1962

Michael and Thomas Asplund launched Asplund as a modern furniture gallery in 1990. Asplund brings a unique perspective to rugs, since the brothers come from a background of furniture and product design rather than from textile design or the traditional carpet trade. Their familiarity with the cutting edge of contemporary furniture, which is largely manufactured in Milan, has given them access to a group of designers who might not otherwise be involved in designing rugs. This group includes names such as Tom Dixon, Jasper Morrison, Marc Newson and Lloyd Schwan, as well as a stable of leading Swedish designers, among them Jonas Brolin and Pia Wallen. This detachment from the traditional areas of the rug market, however, means that all Asplund's rugs are produced using the gun-tufting technique as opposed to traditional techniques such as handknotting.

Battilossi & Kolahi, Editori Italiani di Tappeti
Turin, Italy
Maurizio Battilossi
Born Italy
Behrouz Kolahi
Born Iran, 1954

Maurizio Battilossi and Behrouz Kolahi (shown above) are partners in the Turin-based firm of Battilossi & Kolahi, Editori Italiani di Tappeti. Both coming from the rarefied world of antique rugs and textiles, the pair established the company in the late 1990s to specialize in high-quality contemporary production. The attention to detail and quality that is a requirement of working at the top end of any market is apparent in the carefully selected and meticulously produced designs that they offer. All design work is undertaken in Italy, with production based in Nepal.

Stella Benjamin
Born UK, 1933

Benjamin is almost unique in the world of rugs in that she is one of only a few artists whose rugs are produced by their own hand. After moving to St Ives, Cornwall, in 1956, she quickly became familiar with the prolific and diverse artistic community that still exists there today. Working as an assistant to the sculptor Dennis Mitchell and decorating pottery during the 1960s, Benjamin made an important change of direction in 1967, when she went to work with Bryan Ilsley and Breon O'Casey, this time making jewellery. It was during this period that her interest in weaving began, and after working in this area for several years with O'Casey she established her own weaving studio in 1977. Working exclusively on a Navajo loom and dyeing all her own yarns, including goat's hair, Benjamin designs on the loom, and does not base her pieces on drawings or cartoons. In this respect she is a true artist, as she will not modify colour or scale to suit the needs of an interior. In fact, she does not accept commissions at all. What you see is what you get, and quite exceptional it is, too. Benjamin has exhibited consistently throughout Britain, including shows at the Crafts Council, London, and in 1997 was shortlisted for the prestigious Jerwood Prize. She continues to live and work in St Ives.

Tony Bevan
Born UK, 1951

Tony Bevan trained at Goldsmiths College and the Slade School of Fine Art, both colleges of the University of London. Since the early 1980s he has shown consistently in Britain, Germany and the United States, and he is widely represented in art museums throughout the world. Some critics regard his work as difficult, as it deals with human isolation and psychic disturbance, but most would say it goes beyond fashion and can be ranked only with the most serious and influential artists of our time, such as Francis Bacon and Anselm Kiefer. Bevan makes his paintings on the floor using various charcoals and water-based acrylic paint. This is a highly physical activity, and the idea of a rug being based on his series of *Rafters* paintings, and then being placed on the floor, has exquisite appeal for the artist. Tony Bevan is represented by the London-based dealer Michael Hue-Williams.

Kate Blee
Born UK, 1961

Blee has come to be one of the most highly regarded textile artists of her generation. Graduating from Edinburgh University in 1984, she went on to set up a studio in London. She was the first artist to be commissioned by Christopher Farr of London in 1998 and continues to work with the company today. As well as producing highly regarded rug designs, Blee also works in other media from textile paintings to producing her own line of blankets in Wales and design work for the fashion company Paul Smith. Exhibitions include several shows at the innovative London shop Egg and her work has been purchased by the likes of Giorgio Armani and Donna Karan. Blee's work is in private and public collections including the Crafts Council of Great Britain, the Victoria and Albert Museum, London, and the Contemporary Art Society, London.

Alighiero Boetti
Born Italy, 1940–1994

The late Alighiero Boetti is now beginning to be regarded as one of Italy's most important twentieth-century artists. Arte Povera (Impoverished Art) was the name given to the work of a group of Italian artists who rose to prominence in the late 1960s and 1970s, Boetti being one of their number. In the early 1970s he went to Afghanistan and embraced a culture that had absolutely no interest in the concerns of the Western art world. Indeed, this indifference was echoed by the art world of the United States and Europe, which seemed to have no interest in any culture other than its own. Boetti's best-known works are his camouflage cloth series, his political maps of the world embroidered by women from Afghanistan, and the fifty kilims made by Afghanis based in Pakistan. He has been shown all over the world, most recently at the Whitechapel Art Gallery, London, in 1999, and at the Gagosian Gallery, New York. There is now an Alighiero Boetti archive in Rome.

Chuck Close
Born USA, 1940

American artist Chuck Close has been a leading figure in the contemporary art scene since the early 1970s. He is described as a Photorealist, and his subject-matter is exclusively portraits, or, more accurately, the human face, enormous in size and immensely powerful in effect. Close can make a painting with thousands of minute airbrush bursts or brushstrokes. This technical mastery is akin to the thousands of hand knots tied to warp strings to make a rug, and the artist was naturally delighted to design for such a medium. He is represented in all the major American museums and has had numerous shows throughout the world, including an important exhibition at the Museum of Modern Art, New York, in 1998.

Galerie Diurne Paris, France
Marcel Zelmanovitch
Born France, 1951

Zelmanovitch was one of the first to develop contemporary rug designs in the now saturated production area of Nepal. When he first visited the country in the 1980s, very little innovative design was being produced there, and its main concern was commercial production for the department-store market. His background as an artist and the potential of Nepal as a weaving centre encouraged him to set up his own operation, Galerie Diurne, in Paris. The business oversees an operation that organizes the whole process – spinning, dyeing, weaving and washing – under one roof. This arrangement has significant advantages for controlling quality, a very important factor since a large proportion of the business is involved in custom orders for some of the world's leading interior designers and architects. The design side is run from Paris, with Zelmanovitch responsible for all the artwork. Today Galerie Diurne enjoys continued success as one of the most established and innovative companies at the forefront of the current boom in contemporary rugs and carpets.

Elson & Co. San Francisco, USA
Diane Elson
Born USA, 1971

Diane Elson has a background in antique Oriental carpets and architecture. She founded the San Francisco-based company that carries her name in 1995 after a trip to

Nepal, where she became interested in the by now well-established carpet-weaving industry. As well as designing their own collection, Elson and her partner Nicole Lincoln collaborate with US-based artists and architects to produce collections aimed at both private clients and interior designers. One of the few companies working exclusively in contemporary rugs, Elson & Co. has had considerable success in an increasingly competitive field. Examples of the company's work are included in the permanent collection of the San Francisco Museum of Modern Art.

Christopher Farr London, UK
Christopher Farr
Born UK, 1953
Matthew Bourne
Born UK, 1960

Christopher Farr (shown above, top) trained as a fine artist at Chelsea School of Art and the Slade School of Fine Art, both in London. A trip to Peru in the 1970s triggered an interest in pre-Columbian textiles that led to a passion for tribal weaving and the possibilities of combining this ancient art form with the artistic sensibilities of twentieth-century painting. In 1988 he established the Christopher Farr company with Matthew Bourne (shown above), who shares his passion for carpets and has worked in the trade since leaving school. After an initial period, during which a collection of carpets designed by Farr was sold alongside high-quality antiques, the company collaborated in 1991 with the

Royal College of Art, London. Together they mounted an exhibition of rugs designed by the college's textiles students, entitled *Brave New Rugs*. The instant success of this show convinced Farr and Bourne that the future lay in new production, and they went on to devote all their energy and resources to enhancing the profile and status of the contemporary rug. Today Farr continues to design collections of rugs that reflect his diverse influences, particularly abstract American painting, and the company collaborates with the world's leading artists, architects and designers to push back the boundaries of a field in which it has established itself at the leading edge.

Fort Street Studio Hong Kong, China
Brad Davis
Born USA, 1942
Janis Provisor
Born USA, 1946

This husband-and-wife team, both established artists in the United States with work in numerous private and public collections, became involved in the rug business by chance after a trip to China in the early 1990s. Having found a source for the production of handknotted silk carpets, they set about moulding this to their needs, which were particularly stringent since, as artists, they are used to having complete control over the artistic process. A year and a half was spent on research and development before the launch of their first collection in 1997. Today Fort Street Studio has a growing international reputation for both the originality of its designs and the incredible technical expertise that the work requires. This has been achieved so quickly because of Davis and Provisor's willingness to live in the area of production and ensure that their exacting standards are met. They plan to return from Hong Kong to New York and establish an American base in the near future.

Romeo Gigli
Born Italy, 1949

The Milan-based designer Romeo Gigli is widely regarded within the fashion and textiles industry as one of the greatest colourists in the world today. He began, however, by studying architecture, after which he travelled widely, learning about other art forms and the cultures that had generated them. These experiences inform his distinctive and widely acclaimed fashion collections, which have made him an international figure. In 1993 the London-based rug company of Christopher Farr approached Gigli with a commission to design a series of flatweaves. The resulting collection was first presented in that year at the Salon del Mobile in Milan, to critical acclaim. Given the plethora of fashion designers now turning their attention to home furnishings, Gigli's collection was well ahead of its time.

Allegra Hicks
Born Italy, 1961

Allegra Tondato was born in Turin, Italy, and grew up in a glass house designed by her father and inspired by the buildings of Frank Lloyd Wright. After studying design in Milan and fine art in Brussels, she worked for a contemporary art gallery in New York and then assisted artist Donald Baechler. In 1987 she moved to London to begin her career painting frescoes, and in 1990 married designer Ashley Hicks. Allegra Hicks is primarily a successful textile and fashion designer whose chief – and internationally well-received – contribution to rug design has been her three flatweave collections. Many of the world's most influential designers have commissioned Hicks, whose earthy fields of colour integrate effortlessly with patterns of abstracted natural forms. These designs betray her deep passion for Renaissance painting and the textiles of India.

Gary Hume RA
Born UK, 1962

After graduating from Goldsmiths College, University of London, in 1988, Hume took part in the ground-breaking exhibition *Freeze*, in London, curated by Damien Hirst. Since then he has become one of today's most celebrated artists. He represented Britain at the São Paulo Biennale, Brazil, in 1996 and in the same year was shortlisted for the Turner Prize. In 1997 he was awarded another of Britain's prestigious awards, the Jerwood Prize. By any standard 1999 was an epic year for the artist: he represented Britain in the 48th Venice Biennale and followed this with an important show at the Dean Gallery in the Scottish National Gallery of Modern Art, Edinburgh. In November of the same year he exhibited at London's Whitechapel Art Gallery. As a self-confessed 'beauty terrorist' Hume has said: "I like decoration … . Even if the decoration is benign, you keep on noting in your head that it is actually incredibly luscious and not a cause of anguish … . There's a certain horror in decoration … . It's horrific to know that we can find decoration beautiful, but then it's delicious to know that we can." Hume has brought to the seductive medium of rugs a thoughtful and ironic stance, creating beautiful and typically enigmatic work.

Sandy Jones
Born UK, 1946

During the 1960s Jones worked extensively in the film and fashion industries, which often involved the employment of textiles. A director of the highly regarded yet discreet interior-design practice Chester Jones Ltd, based in London, she has, since the early 1990s, been designing carpets for the interior schemes created by the company as well as working independently to commission. These carpets are, in many cases, very large, and are thought through to the last detail so that they blend smoothly with the accompanying furniture and fabrics, which are also often designed by the company. Owing to the private nature of this work, Jones's carpets are rarely seen by the public, but in 1994 the London-based rug company Christopher Farr staged an exhibition of her work at the Royal College of Art, London.

Kappa Lambda London, UK
Janette Harris
Born UK, 1957
Aman Kanwar
Born India, 1958

Aman Kanwar and Janette Harris founded Kappa Lambda in 1992 and were firmly established as producers of contemporary rugs well before the current craze for modern design. The company produces gun-tufted rugs in its own factory and works with a broad range of designers, including textiles artist Susan Absolon and architect Nigel Coates. Kappa Lambda has also produced a range of needlepoint rugs that are made using worsted wool from Australia. The rugs are mainly sold by such stores as Purves & Purves, but commissions are taken for one-off pieces.

Jan Kath Carpets Bochum, Germany
Jan Kath
Born Germany, 1972

Jan Kath comes from a background steeped in the tradition of handknotted carpets. His father and grandfather built a successful business trading in traditional Oriental carpets in the important German market. After working in the family firm, looking after quality control for some of the new production in Nepal, Kath set up his own company in 1995, continuing to use Nepal as his production base. Kath designs both of his company's lines, one of which updates traditional motifs and designs by using contemporary layouts and colourways, while the other focuses on developing new ideas based around high-quality materials, finishing techniques such as clipping and carving, and the use of bold and subdued monotones. Kath demonstrates a shrewd understanding of the market when he says, "My carpets should not push themselves to the fore, they should not be loud. They should subordinate themselves to the interior but stand confidently for themselves."

Precious McBane London, UK
Meriel Scott
Born Scotland, 1969
Evlynn Smith
Born Scotland, 1962

Scottish artist-designers Evlynn Smith and Meriel Scott have collaborated, under the name Precious McBane, on a remarkable variety of projects since 1993. Both artists studied sculpture at Central St Martin's

College of Art and Design, London, and on graduating they decided to bring much-needed glamour and humour to the well-behaved British design scene. They refuse to work exclusively in any one discipline, preferring to roam freely across interior and set design, fine art and furniture design. Many important seating commissions have been undertaken, for clients such as Prince, Walt Disney and Paul Smith. Several pieces of furniture have been put into production, including the Mongolian beanbag, made infamous when Kate Moss draped herself over one for a UK *Vogue* cover shoot. Current projects include interior colour forecasting for Mix and stage sets for the play *Taranta* by actor-writer Eric von Bargen. In 1997 Smith and Scott received the Best New Designers award at the International Contemporary Furniture Fair (ICFF) in New York. Their rugs encapsulate beautifully their main concerns "to design, disrupt and delight".

Sarah Morris
Born UK, 1967

UK-born American Sarah Morris lives in New York and London and is largely a self-taught artist, having attended only one year of the Whitney Museum of American Art's independent study programme. Her paintings and films can be humorous and are intellectually challenging, inviting us to explore with her the thrilling visual overload of the city and its cultural implications. Her images work on both formal and ideological levels. Morris has brought her exacting and questioning approach to the process of rug design, and while she is concerned with more than mere decoration, she is also clearly delighted with the alluring power of the textile placed on the floor. In 1999 she exhibited at the Museum of Modern Art, Oxford, in 2000 at White Cube, London, the Kunsthalle, Zürich, and the Philadelphia Museum of Art, and in 2001 at Friedrich Petzel, New York, and the National Gallery, Berlin.

Nicholls New York, USA
David Shaw Nicholls
Born Scotland, 1959

David Shaw Nicholls is based in New York City, where he designs and markets rug collections under the Nicholls brand, which has showrooms in New York and Miami FL. After completing studies in furniture design at Edinburgh College of Art in 1976, he moved around the world of design, visiting the United States and, most notably, spending four years in Milan, where he worked for the distinguished designer Ettore Sottsass as project architect at the seminal design practice Sottsass Associati. He took up rug design in 1994 after a fruitless search for a rug to include in one of his projects. Today he produces annual collections, often combining interesting and diverse techniques with a simple and contemporary palette. Nicholls rugs are all hand-made, mostly in Nepal, with finishing work carried out in Europe.

Olly & Suzi
Both born UK, 1968

These two artists are unusual in the contemporary art world for their long collaboration and their subject-matter. Collaboration is rare enough in art, and nearly always lasts only for a short time. Since their time at Central St Martin's College of Art and Design in London, and Syracuse University, New York, they have worked together, showing consistently in Europe and the United States, and most recently at the Natural History Museum, London. Most of their work is done in extremis, in front of wild or endangered animals in remote parts of the world. Paintings are done in situ and simultaneously documented using film and photography. They have made four films: *Raw* (1998), *Ellesmere Island* (1998), *Instinct* (1999) and *Galapagos* (2000). The last of these documents the artists making a painting of turtles moving across the Galapagos sands, which subsequently

became the starting-point for a rug design (see p. 154). It seems fitting to create an object that belongs on the floor to echo the turtles' relationship with the earth.

The Rug Company London, UK
Christopher Sharp
Born UK, 1960
Susan Sharp
Born Malta, 1961

Christopher Sharp established The Rug Company in London in 1997 as a retailer of all types and styles of handwoven rug. Recently the company has followed the trend of working with fashion designers as a means of bringing new ideas to an old tradition, most notably with Consuelo Castiglioni, the designer behind the fashion company Marni, and with Paul Smith. The Rug Company has also produced ranges by such well-known interior designers as Nicky Haslam and Emily Todhunter. As is the case with most companies that are involved in contemporary production, the rugs are woven in Nepal.

Michael Sodeau
Born UK, 1969

A graduate of Central St Martin's College of Art and Design in London, Michael Sodeau is one of Britain's leading designers, working in a variety of fields including furniture, rugs, lighting and ceramics. In 1994 he co-founded the ground-breaking product-design company Inflate, leaving in 1997 to set up his own design studio in partnership with Lisa Giuliani. His point of departure is always the consumer, and the way in which he or she lives with the product. Sodeau's work in rugs is characterized by rigorous thinking that involves every aspect of production, and typically creates innovative results. The Victoria and Albert Museum in London holds work by Sodeau in its permanent collection, and his designs are available in the most interesting and exclusive shops in Europe, Japan and the United States.

Agneta Svensk
Born Sweden, 1952

Swedish-born Agneta Svensk was brought up in the province of Dalarna, which is rich in folkloric traditions. It was here that she apprenticed herself to local craftspeople to learn about working with wool and related skills. After studying at two important weaving schools in Stockholm, Handarbetets Vanner and Wålstedts Textilverkstad, she embarked on a series of journeys to study the culture and textiles of South America, Japan and the Near East. These encounters have had an important influence on her work. Svensk has designed extensively for IKEA as well as working on several other corporate commissions. Most recently she produced her own collection of rugs in Konya, Turkey, and these have been exhibited under the title *Ariadne's Thread* in Sweden, at the Museum of Cultural History, Lund, the Swedish Museum of Textile History, Borås, and the Museum of Mediterranean and Near Eastern Antiquities, Stockholm.

Gavin Turk
Born UK, 1967

Gavin Turk is a graduate of Chelsea College of Art and Design, London, but not the Royal College of Art, where he famously failed his master's degree for showing insufficient work. Ironically, this event launched his celebrated career, mainly as a result of the publicity created by the single exhibit in his degree show, a blue ceramic

plague that read "Borough of Kensington/ Gavin Turk/Sculptor/worked here 1989–1991", a rebellious and humorous comment on the myth of the artist celebrity: a memorial, perhaps, to the demise of art. Turk is an astute observer of the art world and has a shrewd understanding of how the meaning of an art object can be transformed when the work is placed in a new context. By taking his infamous ceramic plaque 'relic' off the wall and placing it on the floor – albeit as a handknotted rug in a larger size – Turk presents another and provocative way of looking at a rug as a conveyor of ideas. Turk has been linked (mainly by the press) with the so-called YBAs (Young British Artists). He is represented in many important public collections, including those of the British Council and the Saatchi Gallery, both London, and the American Federation of Arts, New York.

Veedon Fleece London, UK
Adam M.R. Gilchrist
Born UK, 1959

Adam Gilchrist began his career in the Oriental carpet department at Sotheby's in London, where he developed a passion for handmade rugs. Gilchrist stands out from others in the field in that his starting point as a producer of contemporary rugs lies in a specific desire to help Tibetan refugees in Nepal. He established his weaving facility in the early 1990s and works directly with the weavers, eschewing any temptation to sub-contract to other workshops. This gives him a high degree of control over the product but also brings great risks. Moreover, Gilchrist has taken direct responsibility for the welfare of the families involved in the enterprise, not only in terms of their employment but also through organizing educational and social programmes. Gilchrist brings out two collections each year, one of which is contemporary, and can produce carpets of vast size. The company has recently broken new ground by producing a range of pashmina carpets.

Yukinori Yanagi
Born Japan, 1959

Yukinori Yanagi graduated from Musashino Art University, Tokyo, and then gained a master's degree in fine art at Yale University, in the United States. His highly personal and often controversial work reveals the complexity of being both

Japanese and a contemporary artist. Yanagi explores issues of personal and cultural identity and political and social change in post-war Japan. He is perhaps the most significant and influential Japanese artist of his generation. Yanagi's work has been widely exhibited throughout Asia, Europe, and more recently the United States. His *hinomaru* illumination (1993), a flashing neon billboard of the Japanese flag, appeared in the exhibition *Scream against the Sky: Japanese Art after 1945* at the Guggenheim Museum, New York, in 1994. Continuing his cultural theme in 1995, Yanagi exhibited *The Chrysanthemum Carpet* at the Peter Blum Gallery, New York, in a site-specific installation, finding the medium appropriate for conveying his ideas by means of a huge field of red wool.

Michael Young
Born UK, 1966

British designer Michael Young studied furniture and product design at Kingston University, after which he worked for Tom Dixon at Space UK. In 1994 he opened his own studio, My-022 UK, which he moved to Iceland when he married an Icelandic woman in 1999, renaming it My Studio Ehf. He has designed products for important Italian manufacturers, including Cappellini, Magis, and Sawaya & Moroni. Young is one of the first designers able and good enough to take advantage of the opportunities opened up by Philippe Starck. Following Starck's lead, it is now quite acceptable to design anything from a dog kennel to a computer game. Rugs interest Young insofar as they employ an ancient technology, in contrast to cutting-edge furniture manufacturing. He has little time for the computer-only approach to design; we are, he says, "non-virtual people living in a non-virtual world". Designing a rug is pleasing for that reason alone. Young's products are in the Design Museum, London, the Musée des Arts Décoratifs, Paris, and Die Neue Sammlung, Munich.

PUBLIC MUSEUMS AND GALLERIES

BELGIUM

The Brangwyn Museum
Arents House
Dijver 16
8000 Bruges

Museum of Decorative Arts and Design
Jan Breydelstraat 5
9000 Ghent

CANADA

The Montreal Museum of Fine Arts
1379 Sherbrooke Street West
Montreal
Quebec H3G 2T9

Royal Ontario Museum
100 Queens Park
Toronto
Ontario M5S 2C6

DENMARK

Dansk Kunstindustrimuseum
(The Danish Museum of Decorative Arts)
Bredgade 68
1260 København

FRANCE

Musée des Arts Décoratifs
Palais du Louvre
107 rue de Rivoli
75001 Paris

Musée des Beaux-Arts
1 rue Fernand-Rabier
45000 Orléans

Musée Nationale d'Art Moderne
13 avenue du Président Wilson
75191 Paris

GERMANY

Museum für Völkerkunde
(Museum of Ethnology)
Binderstrasse 14
2000 Hamburg

NORWAY

Kunstindustrimuseet
(Museum of Decorative Arts)
St Olavsg. 1
0165 Oslo

SWEDEN

Moderna Museet
Skeppsholmen
103 27 Stockholm

Röhsska Konstlöjdmuseet
(Röhss Museum of Applied Art & Design)
Vasagatan 37–39
400 15 Göteborg

UK

Victoria and Albert Museum
Cromwell Road
London SW7 2RL

Whitworth Art Gallery
University of Manchester
Oxford Road
Manchester M15 6ER

USA

American Craft Museum
40 West 53rd Street
New York, NY 10019

Drexel University Museum Collection
32nd and Chestnut Streets
Philadelphia, PA 19104

The Metropolitan Museum of Art
The Antonio Ratti Textile Centre
Fifth Avenue at 82nd Street
New York, NY 10028

Museum of Modern Art
11 West 53rd Street
New York, NY 10019

The Textile Museum
2320 S Street, N.W.
Washington, DC 20008–4088

COMMERCIAL GALLERIES AND SHOPS

BELGIUM

Van Caster
Yzerenleen 4–6
Mechelen 2800

CHINA

Fort Street Studio
Harbor Industrial Estate
Unit 1416
10 Lee Hing Street
Ap Lei Chau
Hong Kong

DENMARK

Paustian AS
Kalkbränderilobskaj 2
2100 København

FINLAND

Artek
Södra Esplanaden 18
001 30 Helsingfors

FRANCE

Galerie Diurne
45 rue Jacob
75006 Paris

Galerie Triff
35 rue Jacob
75006 Paris

Roger Misraki
39 rue Grignan
13006 Marseille

Tisca France
Mortières
Route de Cercot
71390 Moroges

GERMANY

Böhmler im Tal
Tal 12
80331 München

Einrichtungshaus Blennenmann
Brueckstraße 59–63
44787 Bochum

Einrichtungshaus Helberger
Große Friedbergerstraße 23
60313 Frankfurt am Main

Galerie Osteler
Ludwigstraße 11
80539 München

Grippekoven & Söhne
Residenzstraße 27
80333 München

H.G. Gunther Teppich & Gardinenhaus
41 Rheinstraße 29
12161 Berlin

Jan Kath Carpets
Bongardstraße 30
44787 Bochum

Kröll & Nill
Zeuggaße 11
86150 Augsburg

Mehner Teppich & Gardinen
Grevesmuhlener Straße 22
13059 Berlin

Mobel Hubner
Genthinerstraße
10785 Berlin

Nyhues Internationale Teppichkollektion
Krahnstraße 20
49074 Osnabrück

Orientteppich West
Maarweg 68
50933 Köln

Riedel Teppiche & Gardinen
Hindenburgdamm 86
12203 Berlin

Schildknecht & Rall & Gerber
Kriegsbergstraße 40–42
70174 Stuttgart

Teppichforum Siegen
Sandstraße 31
57001 Siegen

Teppichhaus Küstermann
Ostwall 16
47798 Krefeld

Teppich Hellriegel
Adolf-Kolping-Straße 177
67433 Neustadt

Ullmann-Teppiche
Langestraße 91
26122 Oldenburg

ITALY
Casa Look
Via Valdera P. 65
56038 Ponsacco (Pisa)

Casa del'Tappezzerie dell'Orto
Via Trabattoni 39
20038 Seregno (Milano)

Centro Veronese del Salotto
Via Dossi
37058 Sanguinetto (VR)

Gemignani Arreda per Ragazzi
Via Valdera P. 65
56088 Ponsacco (Pisa)

Mandarini Arredamenti
Via Ferriera 52
06089 Torgiano (PG)

Meozzi Mobili
Via Roma 4
06010 Pistrino-Citerna (PG)

Morris & Co
Showroom
Corso M. d'Azeglio 20a
10125 Torino

Nilufar
Via Della Spiga 32
20121 Milano

Ottoman Art
Via della Sposa
06123 Perugia

Salina Albera Arredamenti
Via Mambretti 29
20137 Milano

Daniele Sevi
6 via Fiori Chiari
20121 Milano

Stuarr / Vivere Naturale
Via Gregorio VII 307
00165 Roma

Tappeti Contemporanei
Via San Carpoforo 1
20121 Milano

Temacasa
Via Satrico 13c
00183 Roma

LGZ Zanaga
Via Baccio de Montelupo 14
50142 Firenze

Zucchini Arredamenti
Via A. Sandrelli 31
52042 Camuccia di Cortona

NORWAY
Galleri Dobag
Åsveien 38
V/Stasjonen
1369 Stabekk

SWEDEN
Galleri Asplund
Sibyllegatan 31
114 42 Stockholm

NK/Kasthall
Hamngatan 18–20
111 47 Stockholm

Carl Malmstens
Strandvägen 5b
114 51 Stockholm

Svenskt Tenn
Strandvägen 5
114 84 Stockholm

J.P. Willborg
Sibyllegatan 41
114 42 Stockholm

UK
ABC Carpets at Harrods
Harrods
Knightsbridge
London SW1X 7XL

The Alternative Flooring Company
3b Stephenson Close
Andover SP10 3RU

Amazed
Tanfield House
Wighill Village
Nr York
North Yorkshire LS24 8BQ

David Black
27 Chepstow Place
Chepstow Corner
London W2 4TT

Conran Shop
Michelin House
81 Fulham Road
London SW3 6RD

David Gill Galleries
60 Fulham Road
London SW3 6HH

Designers' Guild
269–277 King's Road
London SW3 5EN

Dyson Ringrose Ltd
331 King's Road
London SW3 5ES

Fairman Carpets
118 Westbourne Grove
London W11 2RH

Christopher Farr
212 Westbourne Grove
London W11 2RH

Habitat
196 Tottenham Court Road
London W1T 7LG

Heal & Son Ltd
196 Tottenham Court Road
London W1T 7LQ

Gabriele Herzog
82 Drayton Road
London NW10 4EL

Allegra Hicks
Unit 27
Chelsea Harbour Design Centre
London SW10 0XE

Hill & Co.
Boxhill Road
Boxhill
Surrey KT20 7JE

Tracy Hillier
134 Wynford Road
Islington
London N1 9SW

Paul Hughes Fine Arts
3a Pembridge Square
London W2 4EW

C. John Carpets
70 South Audley Street
London W1K 2RA

Lisa Jones
Studio 2
26–28 Havelock Walk
Forest Hill
London SE23 3HG

Kappa Lambda
Unit 8
Kentish Town Business Park
Regis Road
London NW5 3EW

Keshishian Antique Carpets
73 Pimlico Road
London SW1 8NE

Liberty
210–220 Regent Street
London W1R 6AH

Little & Collins
Units 2–10, Oxo Tower
Barge House Street
London SE1 9PH

Loop House
88 Southwark Bridge Road
London SE1 OEX

Lesley Miller
Little Hoads
Crouch Lane
Sandhurst
Kent TN18 5PA

Annette Nix
Top Flat
11 Estelle Road
London NW3 2JK

Roger Oates Design Co. Ltd
The Long Barn
Eastnor
Ledbury
Herefordshire HR8 1EL

Orientalist
152–154 Walton Street
London SW3 2JJ

Purves & Purves
220–224 Tottenham Court Road
London W1T 7QE

The Rug Company
124 Holland Park Avenue
London W11 4UE

Annie Sherburne Rugs
179a Goldhurst Terrace
London NW6 3ER

Skandium
72 Wigmore Street
London W1U 2SG

Stark Carpet
Chelsea Harbour Design Centre
London SW10 0XE

Robert Stephenson
1 Elystan Street
London SW3 3NT

Stockwell Carpets
24 Harcourt Street
London W1H 1DT

Topfloor
Chelsea Harbour Design Centre
London SW10 0XE

Tribe
52 Cross Street
London N1 2BA

Christine Van Der Hurd
2 Ruston Mews
London W11 1RB

Veedon Fleece
42 Nightingale Road
Guilford
Surrey GUI IEP

V'Soske
Unit 16
The Coda Centre
189 Munster Road
London SW6 6AW

Helen Yardley
A–Z Studios
3–5 Hardwidge Street
London SE1 3SY

USA

ABC Carpet & Home
881/888 Broadway at East 19th Street
New York, NY 10003

A/D
560 Broadway
New York, NY 10012

Angela Adams
273 Congress Street
Portland, ME 04101

David E. Adler
6990 East Maine Street
Scottsdale, AZ 85251

Balentine Carpets International
533 East Hopkins Avenue
Aspen, CO 81611

Birmingham Contemporary Design Center, Inc.
2817 6th Avenue South
Birmingham, AL 35233

Casa Décor
720 Dallas Design Center
1025 North Stemmons Freeway
Dallas, TX 75207

Elson & Company
3723 Sacramento Street
San Francisco, CA 94118

Entrée Libre
110 Wooster Street
New York, NY 10012

Christopher Farr
Courtyard Gallery
748 North La Cienega Boulevard
Los Angeles, CA 90069

F.J. Hakimian
136 East 57th Street
2nd Floor
New York, NY 10022

De Sousa Hughes
S.F.D.C. Showplace
2 Henry Adams Street
Suite 220
San Francisco, CA 94103

Limn
290 Townsend Street
San Francisco, CA 94107

Michaelian & Kohlberg
578 Broadway
Suite 201
New York, NY 100122

Dennis Miller Associates
New York Design Center
200 Lexington Avenue
Suite 1510
New York, NY 10016

Nicholls New York
578 Broadway
16th Floor
New York, NY 10012

Odegard, Inc.
New York Design Center
200 Lexington Avenue
Suite 1206
New York, NY 10016

Ralph Pucci
44 West 18th Street
New York
NY 10011

Ralph Pucci @Thomas Job
1636 Merchandise Mart
Chicago, IL 60654

Driscoll Robbins
1002 Western Avenue
Seattle, WA 98104

Jeffrey Rogers
902 Broadway
2nd Floor
New York, NY 10010

Stark Carpet
D&D Building
979 Third Avenue
New York, NY 10022

Christine Van Der Hurd
102 Wooster Street
New York, NY 10012

V'Soske, Inc.
155 East 56th Street
New York, NY 10022

Introduction

1. Different terminologies and criteria are applied to the definition of rugs and carpets throughout Europe and the United States. In the United Kingdom, Customs and Excise differentiate on the basis of size: a rug is defined as having dimensions up to 300 × 200 cm (118 × 79 in.), and anything larger is defined as a carpet. Museums in the United Kingdom, however, tend to refer to pieces of any size as carpets. In the United States, a fitted floor covering is referred to as a carpet, and an unfitted weaving as a rug. For the purposes of this essay, I prefer to call most unfitted woven floor-pieces rugs (rug being the original term in Europe for a woven textile that was positioned on the floor, while a carpet was placed on a table). If very large, the piece is referred to as a carpet, and fitted, wall-to-wall woven flooring is referred to as carpeting.

2. *22 Tapijten = 22 Carpets = 22 Teppiche*, exhib. cat., Ghent, Atelier Vermeersch and Galerie Weinand, 1995.

3. Introduction, *International Exhibition: European Glass and Rugs*, exhib. cat., New York, American Federation of Arts, 1929.

4. See Harold Acton, *Memoirs of an Aesthete*, 1948, quoted in C. Boydell, *The Architect of Floors: Modernism, Art and Marion Dorn Designs*, p. 13.

5. Andrée Putman, quoted in *Tapis de création Laine*, trade cat. of Toulemonde Bochart, Paris, 2001.

1900–1909:
New Styles for a New Century

6. Towards the end of the nineteenth century, Italian art and design of the period between the 1300s and the 1600s became a popular subject for study by scholars and aesthetes, and in public museums, and manifested itself in such artistic movements as the Pre-Raphaelites. Far Eastern aesthetics had also been highly influential on the Aesthetic Movement of the 1870s, a fashion that had resulted in Arthur Liberty opening, in 1875, a store selling Eastern fabrics in Regent Street, London. Specializing in textiles, ceramics and objets d'art from Japan and China as well as the Near and Middle East, Liberty was a key

proponent of the latest avant-garde styles such as the Aesthetic, Celtic Revival and Art Nouveau.

7. A stable green dye was difficult to obtain from natural dyes and therefore green tended to be used in small quantities.

8. Quoted in Dun Emer Industries prospectus, 1903.

9. Dun Emer continued to produce rugs until the 1950s.

1910s–1930s:
The Flourishing Years

10. The rug designed by Vanessa Bell for Lady Hamilton is now in the collection of the Victoria and Albert Museum, London (museum no. Circ. E.722–1955), with the original design.

11. See letter from Janet Ashbee to Charles R. Ashbee after she had visited the Omega Workshops in August 1913, published in *The Omega Workshops 1913–19*, exhib. cat., cat. no. M5, London, Crafts Council, 1984.

12. An example of Ambrose Heal's work can be seen at the Victoria and Albert Museum, London (museum no. Circ. 601–1966), machine-woven by Tomkinsons Ltd, 1921.

13. Gordon Russell Ltd, Spring Fabrics leaflet 1934, back page, as published in *Marian Pepler*, exhib. cat., R.D. Russell, London, Geffrye Museum, *et al.*, 1983.

14. Paul Nash designs for Donegal gun-tufted rugs can be seen in the Designs Collection at the Victoria and Albert Museum, London (museum nos. Circ. E.5205 and 5206–1960).

15. 'The 1930 Look in British Decoration', *The Studio*, August 1930.

16. In 1923 the Finn Eliel Saarinen was invited by the American George G. Booth to set up an experimental art community, the Cranbrook Academy of Art, where artists could live and work. Saarinen designed his own landmark house, which was finished in 1930, and beautiful handmade rugs, designed and made by Loja Saarinen, were included in each room. These are some of the most outstanding rugs and carpets made in the United States at this time (and, with the house, have recently been restored).

17. The exhibition of *European Contemporary Glass and Rugs*, New York, 1929.

1940s–1950s:
Austerity and Renewal

18. V'Soske has long been one of the foremost producers of handwoven and (later) gun-tufted rugs and carpets. Started by Stanislav V'Soske (1900–1983) in 1924, it designed and wove the first gun-tufted rugs in the United States, and is best known for high-pile and sculptured and moulded pieces.

1960s–1970s:
Pop, Op and Fun

19. Original label, partly illegible, on the reverse of a Heal & Son Ltd rug of the mid-1960s (fig. 27).

20. *Ryijy: Rugs from Finland*, exhib. cat, Loyola Marymount University Art Gallery, 1983, p. 16.

21. The flatweave *raanu* technique creates a sparse pile and is used for traditional Lapp bed covers.

22. Introduction, *Modern Master Tapestries*, exhib. cat., 1970.

1980s–2001:
Post-modernism, Faith, Craft and a Brave New World

23. See also the *Kloc* 'rest-rug' by Christian Gavoille in wool felt with a foam-filled hump, made for Ligne Roset, 2000, and the 2001 woven rattan, polypropylene and steel *Jari* mat designed by Jihoon Ha in Copenhagen, Denmark.

Abrasch
A word of Turkish origin, meaning 'movement', that describes the myriad variations in tone within a single colour. When this movement is even and subtle it adds greatly to the appeal of a carpet. However, if it is pronounced and there are sharp divisions in tone, it can be considered a fault.

Cartoon
The final rendering of a design, which plots the position of each knot in the carpet, allowing the weaver to follow the designer's intentions much like reading a map. Cartoons are normally produced at one-third of the size of the finished carpet and are placed above the loom in sections, usually two or three per design.

Clipping
A technique that forms part of the finishing process, in which pile height can be altered or decorative effects such as relief patterns can be achieved. This is traditionally carried out by hand, although there are now machines that can perform the task.

Ends
The term used to refer to the rows of wefts at each end of the carpet that provide the same function as the selvedge.

Flatweave
Commonly called a 'kilim', a flatweave is a handloomed product rather like a coarse tapestry. Whereas design and colour in a handknotted rug are created through the pile, in a flatweave these are introduced through packing the wefts tightly over the warps so that the warps are completely hidden and only the weft face is visible.

Gun-tufting
The most common and cheapest form of production currently used in the manufacturing of contemporary rugs. The technique involves 'punching' tufts of coloured yarn into a latex base using a hand-held electronic tool. Artwork can be reproduced to a very high degree of accuracy using this method.

Handknotting
The oldest known method of producing a woven floor covering, dating back many thousands of years to the Near and Far East. The technique involves the knotting of strands of wool around one or two warp threads to form a pile or nap. The knots are built up row upon row and secured by the insertion of wefts.

Handspun wool
The traditional and best way to form a weavable yarn from a woollen fleece. The fleece is held in one hand while a spindle held in the other hand is spun to twist the fibres together. This method causes the fibres to lie parallel with each other, and prevents them from matting, creating a softer, more luxurious pile.

Loop pile
A type of pile-face in which the yarn turns back on itself to leave a loop, as opposed to single strands of yarn forming the pile of the carpet.

Machine-spun wool
The modern and most common method of making yarn from fleece makes use of large machines that do the job far more quickly and economically than handspinning. The disadvantage of this method is that the process strips the yarn of much of its natural protective properties such as lanolin. It also provides a homogeneous product that results in flatter colour when dyed and a more commercial feel.

Mixed technique
A term applied whenever two techniques are employed within the same carpet, such as handknotting and flatweave.

Selvedge
The terms for the edges of a carpet, which have tightly woven wefts interlocking around two or three warps to provide protection for the piled area of the carpet.

Warp
The vertical threads that are stretched on to the loom before the carpet is begun and on to which knots are tied.

Weft
The tightly spun yarn that is inserted between each row of knots, running horizontally across the carpet, to hold the knots in place. By interlocking with the warp, the weft also provides the foundation of the carpet.

22 Tapijten = 22 Carpets = 22 Teppiche, exhib. cat., Ghent, Atelier Vermeersch and Galerie Weinand, 1995

P. Bayer, *Art Deco Source Book: A Visual Reference to a Decorative Style 1920–40*, London 1988

I. Bennett (ed.), *The Country Life Book of Rugs and Carpets of the World*, London 1977

D. Black (ed.), *World Rugs and Carpets*, Feltham 1985

C. Boydell, *Marion Dorn: The Architect of Floors*, exhib. cat., London, RIBA, 1996

British Art and Design 1900–1960, London 1983

M. Byars, *The Design Encyclopedia*, New York 1994

'Craftsman in style: A biographical sketch of Ronald Grierson, MSIA, one of Britain's most versatile designers', *Furnishing and Design*, III, July–September 1948, pp. 91–94

Dorothy Liebes, exhib. cat., New York, Museum of Contemporary Crafts of the American Crafts Council, 20 March – 10 May 1970

A. Drexler and G. Daniel, *Introduction to Twentieth Century Design from the Collection of the Museum of Modern Art*, New York 1959

C.B. Faraday, *European and American Carpets and Rugs* [1929], Woodbridge 1990

C. Fiell and P. Fiell (eds.), *Decorative Art, 1900s, 1910s: A Source Book*, Cologne 2000

C. Fiell and P. Fiell (eds.), *60s Decorative Art: A Source Book*, Cologne 2000

C. Fiell and P. Fiell (eds.), *70s Decorative Art: A Source Book*, Cologne 2000

For the Floor: An International Exhibition of Contemporary Handmade Rugs, exhib. cat., New York, American Craft Museum II, 1985

M. Ginsburg (ed.), *The Illustrated History of Textiles*, London 1991

M. Haslam, *Arts and Crafts Carpets*, London 1991

M. Haworth-Booth, *E. McKnight Kauffer: A Designer and his Public*, London 1979

R. Horn, *Memphis*, Philadelphia 1985

International Exhibition of Contemporary Glass and Rugs, exhib. cat., New York, American Federation of Arts, 1929

L. Jackson, *The Sixties: Decade of Design Revolution*, London 1998

V. Klint, 'Memories of the Weaver Gerda Henning', *Scandinavian Journal of Design History*, V, 1995

M. Matet, *Tapis Modernes*, Paris 1929

D.R. McFadden, *Scandinavian Modern Design*, New York 1982

D.K. Meilach, *Making Contemporary Rugs and Wall Hangings*, London and New York 1970

The Omega Workshops 1913–1919: Decorative Arts of Bloomsbury, exhib. cat., London, Crafts Council, 1984

B. Radice, *Memphis: Research, Experiences, Results, Failures and Successes of New Design*, London 1985

Rugs, exhib. cat., New York, World House Galleries, 1962

R.D. Russell, *Marian Pepler*, exhib. cat., London, Geffrye Museum; Glasgow, Glasgow Art Gallery and Museum; Leicester, Leicestershire Museum and Art Gallery; Bath, Crafts Study Centre; 1983

Ryijy rugs from Finland, exhib. cat. by A.-L. Amberg and R. Pylkkänen, Helsinki, Museum of Applied Arts; Los Angeles, Loyola Marymount University Art Gallery; 1983

S.B. Sherrill, *Carpets and Rugs of Europe and America*, New York 1996

J. Sirat and F. Siriex, *Tapis français du XXe siècle: de l'art nouveau aux créations contemporaines*, Paris 1993

Six Chairs and Six Rugs, exhib. cat. by S. Roberts, Winchester, The Winchester Gallery, 1991

C.E.L. Tattershall and S.A. Reed, *A History of British Carpets*, rev. and enlarged edn, 1966

Thirties, exhib. cat., London, Arts Council of Great Britain, 1979

H. Wakefield, *Weaving for Walls: Modern British Wall Hangings and Rugs*, London 1970

J.M. Woodham, *Twentieth Century Design*, Oxford 1997

S. Wortmann Weltage, *Bauhaus Textiles: Women Artists and the Weaving Workshop*, London 1993

Websites

www.adgallerynewyork.com
www.albertolevi.com
www.amazed-rugs.co.uk
www.barjischohan.com
www.cfarr.co.uk
www.chichicavalcanti.com
www.fernmark.com
www.fjhakimian.com
www.hillco.co.uk
www.kappa-lambda.co.uk
www.loophouse.com
www.newzealandwool.com
www.teppichsachverstaendiger.de
www.tracyhillier.co.uk
www.veedonfleece.demon.co.uk

The authors would like to offer their grateful thanks to the following for their assistance in the production of this book, and for generously providing access to their collections: Jane Adlin, Curator of Textiles at the Metropolitan Museum of Art, New York, Yael Aloni, Peter Blum, Elisabeth Cunnick, Lieven Daenens, Director of the Ghent Decorative Arts and Design Museum, Stefan Drechsle, Simon Franses, Farhad J. Hakimian, Kate Hume, Pierre Louis Juillet, Arto and Eddie Keshishian, Zoë Kurtz, Alberto Levi, Longevity, Marianne Panton, Andrée Putman, Leon Sassoon, Monika Stadler, Madeline Weinrib, Mel Yates.

Christopher Farr, Matthew Bourne and Fiona Leslie

In writing the contextual essay I have been helped by many people from across Europe and the United States who are passionate about rugs. I should also like to thank Christopher and Matthew for asking me to contribute to this much-needed book and for having the vision and enthusiasm to make it a reality.

In carrying out the research, I was particularly honoured to work with some of the designers themselves and should like to thank Jack Lenor Larsen, Helen Yardley and Baris Chochan for insights into their work.

Colleagues at the Victoria and Albert Museum, London, have been tremendously supportive and my thanks go to Jennifer Wearden for her comments on the early drafts, to Dr Norbert Jopek for translations, and to Susan Lambert, Shaun Cole, Divia Patel, Shashi Sen and Martin Durrant in the Picture Library. The team at Merrell Publishers has been patiently supportive in its guidance.

My friends have been pillars throughout this project and I cannot mention them all, but I would like to send my love to Mary and Bob Sibert, for putting up with me during research in New York, Eleanor Curtis, Mikala Djørup, Dr Andreas Petzold, Luis Santos and Ian McIntyre, and Karina and Raffi Sarkisian.

Fiona Leslie